STORIES ON THE FRONT PORCH

Elmer L. Towns

STORIES ON THE FRONT PORCH

Elmer L. Towns

Regal

A Division of Gospel Light
Ventura, California, U.S.A.

Published by Regal Books
A Division of Gospel Light
Ventura, California, U.S.A.
Printed in U.S.A.

Regal Books is a ministry of Gospel Light, an evangelical Christian publisher dedicated to serving the local church. We believe God's vision for Gospel Light is to provide church leaders with biblical, user-friendly materials that will help them evangelize, disciple and minister to children, youth and families.

It is our prayer that this Regal book will help you discover biblical truth for your own life and help you meet the needs of others. May God richly bless you.

For a free catalog of resources from Regal Books/Gospel Light please contact your Christian supplier or call 1-800-4-GOSPEL.

Library of Congress Cataloging-in-Publication Data
Towns, Elmer L.
Stories on the front porch / Elmer L. Towns.
p. cm.
ISBN 0-8307-1870-2 (hardcover).
1. Towns, Elmer L. 2. Baptists—United States—Biography.
3. Christian educators—United States—Biography. 4. Christian
life—Baptist authors. 5. Conduct of life. I. Title.   96-23998
BX6495.T597A3 1996   CIP

1 2 3 4 5 6 7 8 9 10 11 12 13 14 15 16 17 / 02 01 00 99 98 97 96

Rights for publishing this book in other languages are contracted by Gospel Literature International (GLINT). GLINT also provides technical help for the adaptation, translation and publishing of Bible study resources and books in scores of languages worldwide. For further information, contact GLINT, P.O. Box 4060, Ontario, CA 91761-1003, U.S.A., or the publisher.

Dedicated to Erin McFaddin Towns

A mother who inculcated character in her son,
Who didn't always want it or respond to it;
A mother who had limited resources because
she found herself without money and without a
proper role model for her son;
A mother who overcame difficulties
and insurmountable odds to give her son
an appetite to habitually do the
Right thing in the right way.

Response

I have not always done the right thing in the right way,
None of us have;
But like most of us, I find the fruit of my life
Has grown according to the seeds planted by my parents;
Most of us can't make too many changes in what we are,
But we can plant better seeds in our children.

Contents

Part I: Teachers

Part II: Mother

Part III: Friends

Part IV: Uncles

Part V: Doing Wrong, Naturally

Part VI: Tools that Teach

"Elmer and Erin"

Preface

The Sidewalks of Our Childhood

Money has always influenced me—at least the lack of money. Daddy was a heavy drinker, a compulsive drinker, an alcoholic. He hid his bottle in the hydrangea bush beside the front steps and would not bring it into the house. Why? Mother poured it out when she found it. Sometimes he hid it in the floor joist under the house. It was a pathetic sight to see a grown man crawling under the house because he was scared of his wife. Then he would go back after it later and hide it under his pillow and drink himself to sleep. Mother never tried to physically take a bottle away from him. She sneaked. He sneaked.

Confronting City Hall

My parents argued about money. Mother wanted more money for bills. Daddy spent most of the money on liquor. One day a check came to our house from City Hall. I think it was for $14. I remember Daddy earned $52 a week from White's Hardware, and a quart of liquor cost $5. So a $14 check was a lot of money.

Mother dressed me and left my sister, Martha, with a neighbor. She dressed me in a white shirt and knotted a tie in place. "We've got to look our best," she told me. We caught the trolley car four blocks from our house. Mother dropped an eight-cent token into the box for herself, and because I was a child I rode for half price. She was mad. Although I was only about eight years old, I knew what "mad" meant, and mother was angry. I could feel her irritation all the way to town.

We got off the trolley and walked briskly down Bay Street to City Hall. I remember mother always walked briskly and I had to trot alongside to keep up with her. Mother walked determinedly into the front door of City Hall, her high heels clicking on the marble floor. Every footstep echoed from the rotunda. It was the first time I had been there. The smell of cleaning oil the janitor used to sweep the floor was strange. Mother walked to a window and barked a question to the elderly male clerk,

"Who sent this check to us?" She pointed to the printed word "welfare."

"We're not poor!" she announced for everyone in the office to hear. Apparently, my father had some pull at City Hall and got the Towns name placed on some list so he could receive welfare payments each month. I assume what he did was legal.

"Take our name off that list," mother demanded. "And don't send another one," she concluded with finality. That night mother and father quarreled about the check. To my knowledge, we never received another one.

Teachable Epochs

This experience, like a footprint in wet concrete, is a haunting memory. Some childhood experiences last a lifetime and each time we see the footprint in the sidewalk of life, it reminds us of that original event.

This welfare check was one of those "teachable epochs" of life. I learned "don't be poor" and "work for your money." These are not necessarily biblical values, but they became my values. I also learned "respect for the family name" and "it's important what people think of you so we dress up to make an impression." I also learned, "People think more of those who have money than they do of the poor."

The sidewalks of our childhood stay with us for life because we walk them as adults. From time to time we must intentionally return to them even if only in our minds. The sidewalks of the past help us understand who we are and why we act as we do. By retracing our steps on the sidewalks of our minds, we can better cope with the challenge of our adult experiences.

Living by Principles

I wrote this book, not as memoirs, as some elderly do to attempt reminiscing about the past. My memories have meaning only to me; my experiences have no value to history because my life has been average. I did not write this book to foster a movement, establish an institution or to get even with someone.

I wrote *Stories on the Front Porch* to help you look within so you too can live by principles. I am not saying my principles are better than others, or my life is better than others. I do, however, have some principles that are important to me and I understand how I got them. Although I know these principles, I have fallen short of many of my expectations. In an imperfect world made up of selfish driven people, however, we struggle against seemingly insurmountable odds and with limited resources. Considering this kind of world, I am relatively satisfied because I know a few principles and they guide me through the strange and fearsome sidewalks of life.

I have two confessions about these principles. First, I attempt to please God with my principles, and to the best of my ability, I have tried to attach them to Christian principles. I did not want to try and sneak up on you if you are not a believer in God. My second confession grows out of my belief that no one has perfect knowledge—only God. These principles are not perfect, as much as I want them to be.

As we grow older, we tend to glorify our past and minimize our failures. I have tried to be as accurate as possible. To do that I have had my sister, Martha Sue Akins, and my brother, Richard Towns, read the manuscript to add or take away anything that abridges the truth as they remember it. I have also allowed my wife, Ruth, and children, Debbie, Sam and Polly, the same quality control. I don't, however, pass the buck to them for the weaknesses of this book. I take all responsibility for the mistakes and omissions of this book. May it hurt no one, and help all readers.

My father died at age 64 in 1964 so he had no opportunity to read the manuscript. I could have let my mother read the manuscript, but I didn't because it does not always glamorize her, although she was a great giant. This book presents her realistically as I remember her. Some things she would deny, such as her drinking alcohol—perhaps because after she walked with Christ she turned against alcohol. Because she suffered the consequences of my father's drinking, she does not like to remember that part of her life. In any case, my aunts remember my mother as a flapper of the 1920s who carried her husband's bottle in a paper sack during the prohibition days of her youth.

May God bless these stories to help you establish priorities for your life so you too can have principles to guide your life.

Sincerely yours in Christ,
Elmer L. Towns

"Erin Towns and the crying dog"

Introduction

The Crying Dog: The Hardest Decision of My Life

Persuading Mother to Leave Her House

"I won't go!" my mother said defiantly as I tried to take her gently by the arm. She pulled her arm away and walked out of the hot kitchen into the musty dining room. The house was old with fading blue paint on plaster, although cracked plaster. The house had once been at the end of a dirt street in the country, but now it was on a noisy, busy main thoroughfare and a traffic light stood at the corner. My mother's house was almost as old as she, and was in about the same physical condition. The pounding of hammers all around told of new homes being built close by. The rip of an electric saw reminded us of a new day, while the old refused to pass.

"This is my house and I want to live right here. I don't want to go," Mother said, more fear being reflected in her voice than anger. This former giant of a woman now weighed less than 100 pounds. In my mind she stood taller than all the women in the world; yet she was only five feet one inch tall. For 89 years (at least we allowed her that age, although the family Bible contained a discrepancy), she was as strong as she had to be. She still had the physical stamina to work in her garden each day. She hoed the weeds, and tenderly raised her plants.

I knew the year my mother did not plant her vegetable garden, that would be the year she died. Because life is tied to our dreams and aspirations, Mother lived because she lived for her garden. So in the spring of 1994, just like every other year since I can remember, she planted her eight tomato plants, four rows of new potatoes, radishes, as always, and Kentucky wonders—what most people call string beans, or what we Southerners affectionately call snap beans. This was just her spring garden. Every fall she also planted rows of cabbage, turnips and collard greens, just to mention a few.

Mother's Prize Gardens

Mother was famous in Savannah, Georgia, for her organic garden. She said it was a sin to use commercial fertilizer, so she hired lawn men to bring in a truckload of leaves, then plow them into the ground so when they rotted the soil was provided with life-giving nutrients.

In 1956, Mother bought a house for $4,000. The lot was approximately 100 feet wide, and deep enough to contain two acres. The only problem was that the soil was sandy, and to anyone else it was unfit for nourishing a rich vegetable garden. Not to Erin Towns, though, who loved the soil as she loved her own soul. She not only hauled in the dead leaves and plowed them under, but she also buried most of the garbage from our table into the soil, including egg shells, coffee grounds and potato peels. She once broke down and bought a load of lime. A friend who worked at the Georgia Port Authorities, the seaport for Savannah, brought it and scattered the white film over her garden. As a result, the sandy yard was as porous as any beach on the Atlantic Ocean. Gradually, its black soil became the envy of the neighborhood because it could grow anything.

When I was a little boy, Mother would tell me, "Get your wagon and run get Mr. Brickhoff's leaves," after he raked his yard and put them at the curb for the garbage.

"Mom," I complained, "it's embarrassing to be a garbage man." But she prevailed, and I went to get the leaves. Then with a shovel I buried them under the black sandy soil.

I often said that if Mother planted a hoe handle in the ground, it would grow tomatoes. I came to this conclusion one day while doing my required yard work, digging in the soil, pulling up weeds or picking the tomatoes. I don't remember just when I first said it, but you heard it repeated among our neighbors or relatives: "Erin could grow tomatoes on a hoe handle."

The sandy backyard needing enrichment to grow anything, however, was not Erin's ultimate obstacle. She married Elmer Leon Towns in 1930. The young man who had the brilliant memory was the ordering clerk at White Hardware Company on the corner of Whitacher and Brian Streets in Savannah.

Elmer and Erin: A Beautiful Couple

If ever there was a beautiful couple, Elmer and Erin were the envy of many. Elmer was a snappily dressed young man, had black hair and a job to be envied—during the Depression. Erin was an aggressive, petite, black-haired girl who spent one year at Winthrop College in Rock Hill, South Carolina, then finished the business course at Savannah Business College. Elmer and Erin started out on the top of the heap. They lived in a home 10 miles out in the country near deep salt water, and to complete the picture, they also owned a boat. Elmer drove a Ford roadster—a two-seater sporting a rumble seat. They went dancing, attended the Indy-type auto races that roared in front of their house, and had enough money to take vacations in Myrtle Beach, South Carolina.

Unfortunately, Elmer had a dark demon troubling him—drinking. He liked his liquor and could not say no. After 15 years of marriage, Erin stood in church and wept at a prayer meeting, "I thought when I married him I could keep him from going too far..."

She could do everything, she thought, but she could not keep her husband away from the bottle. Every time they moved, the neighborhood was not quite as nice, and the house was not as modern. Elmer's drinking, like the Empire State Building, was a towering influence in everything he and Erin did. As the marriage grew older, liquor kept them from going places, from having clothes and from buying a new car. Liquor also kept them from having enough food to put on the table.

Maybe that is how the vegetable garden came into being. Erin was raised on a 154-acre tobacco farm in central South Carolina, and she understood the whole world of farming. Her father, Robert Eli McFaddin (a baby boomer born the year after the Civil War), loved the soil that gave life to his family of 11 children. As Erin ran her fingers through the soil of her garden, she gained hope and strength because she was feeding her family from the rows so carefully plowed and watered.

My father once yelled at me when I was a boy, "Get a flashlight and go out and help your mother in the garden." He did not mean it. He was mad because she did not come in to cook supper. She loved her garden more than cleaning, sewing, ironing or anything else, and she never came into the house until all the gardening was done.

Erin looked to the future. She knew that if the garden was not planted in April, no food would be ready for us in July.

Mother's Final Day at Her Beloved Home

Now, tugging at Mother's arm, I was having the toughest day of my life. I was trying to make her leave the house and garden she loved more than life. I was trying to put her into a rest home.

I walked out on the back porch and looked at her garden. Everything was orderly, the rows all exactly the same length. The vegetables needing sun were planted in the sunlight, and those needing shade from the scorching Georgia sun were under the massive live oak tree that grew near the house. Like all good Southern gardens, it was surrounded with wire fencing attached to steel poles. Kentucky wonders (string beans) grew on the sunny side of the fence, just outside the garden. Flowers of all varieties decorated the inside, and Mother could tell you what all of them were, giving their entire pedigree.

Erin Towns's garden was much like her children. She made them grow straight, orderly and produce fruit according to her dominating will. Just as she had turned a sandy backyard into rich loam that produced fruit, so her children produced the fruit of character although they grew up in a home of drunkenness, fierce arguments and severe beatings. She often said, "If you *do* right, you'll *be* right." And she lived to see that all her children inevitably did the right thing.

One day I asked my sister, Martha, why she was always such a good girl and seldom did anything wrong. Martha did not sass her mother, she did not disobey Dad. Outwardly, she was a perfect little girl. In response to my question, Martha answered, "I never had a choice to be bad."

Just as Erin Towns did everything to make her garden productive, so she did everything for her children to make sure they had the best—within her limited circumstances. The best was not always bought with money. It was bought with time, sacrifice and teaching. She was always teaching her children how to *be* right.

Green Acres

On June 15, 1994, Erin Towns had to leave her garden and her house, and enter a professional extended care home; a place where she would receive the care she needed. I had visited the Green Acres Professional Care Home, located only two miles from where my mother had her garden. The St. Augustine grass and beautiful live oak trees at Green Acres were the same as what my mother had in her backyard. She could hear the same sounds from swaying limbs she could hear at home. It was less than a mile from the salt marshes of the ocean, and she could smell the ocean breezes.

Green Acres had originally been a large, four-bedroom private home. It was located on seven acres and surrounded by a six-foot chain link fence for protection. The lawn was beautifully manicured. Best of all, the home was air-conditioned 24 hours a day. Mother had never lived in an air-conditioned home. She never let her children air-condition her house. She complained, "When I was a little girl, I grew up with the weather God gave me. Why should I shut out the outdoors? Why should I breathe that stale air? Why should I get sick from air-conditioning?"

She did allow us to install ceiling fans in every room. Her old house had tall nine-foot ceilings, and the paddle fan stirred up the air. We installed an exhaust fan to pull out the hot air in the kitchen. Still, she went to bed each night in that old house in 75 degree temperature during the summer. And she loved every night she spent there. Green Acres was impeccably clean and modern. It had every appliance in the kitchen, which Mother never had and never wanted. Neither had she ever lived in a place this clean. Not that her house was not passably clean; she just didn't put a lot of emphasis on keeping house. She did not even own a vacuum cleaner. She just swept her house with a broom before the days of electricity, so she continued to do so until the day she moved out. It was her way of doing things in 1914, so why not do the same thing in 1994?

Green Acres was not a nursing home. No invalids occupied the beds, and no bottles and tubes hung from the bedsides. Other women would have paid dearly to move into Green Acres, but not Erin Towns. She wanted her house, her garden and she wanted us to leave her alone. Alzheimer's disease, however, was gnawing away at her like salt water gnawing away a metal chain, so her mind was losing its effectiveness, event by event, and date by date. She said something to us, then repeated it 10 times, each time forgetting she had already said it earlier.

Mother's Alzheimer's Regression

Mother went to see the doctor, and he prescribed Cognac for her, which was the latest "cutting edge" miracle drug to help Alzheimer's patients. But we all knew that Cognac could not reverse Alzheimer's. The only thing the doctor promised us was that it would arrest the disease's progress. At $10 a pill, or $110 a bottle, it was a price we wanted to pay—had to pay—to help Mother's mind remain the great mind that had guided our childhood.

On June 15, Mother kept offering reasons why she did not want to go to Green Acres Home.

"Get Mrs. Barnes to come stay with me," she pleaded.

"Get Laurine to come and stay with me," she said.

We had been searching for six months for someone to stay with Mother, and had talked to everyone she suggested. They could not possibly do what she wanted them to do, and what needed to be done. Alzheimer's requires constant care, 24-hours-a-day care.

"I'll go live with Richard and Jackie," she pled. Richard, her youngest child, had been fixing up a room for her and he agreed to take her in to live there. Richard and Jackie, however, both worked outside the home every day. They had three kids in public schools and one in college. They could not give Mother the constant care she needed around the clock.

One night she packed her suitcase, called Richard, and asked him to come get her immediately. He found her going out the front door to move down the street to her new house.

There was no new house. Perhaps she was thinking of 1938, when she moved from Adair Street to Wagner Street a couple of blocks away.

One morning she demanded that Richard come over and get the horse out of the garden. The horse was eating her vegetables. When Richard arrived, he saw no horse. He tried to tell her there was no horse, but by then she did not remember the episode. She claimed she never said anything about the horse, and got mad when Richard tried to convince her he was right.

Apparently, when Mother was a very young girl, a horse had come into the garden and some emotional imprinting was attached to that event. She never forgot it, and the memory was close at hand ready to be revived in her old age.

We thought we had prepared Mother for her move to Green Acres. My wife and I had visited the home and found it completely satisfactory. We had checked out the kitchen, laundry, the room where she would be staying and all financial details. Then I brought my brother, Richard, and my sister, Martha. They agreed: The home was perfect.

Then we brought Mother there and showed her the place. We walked her through and showed her the room where she would be staying. Next we walked into the great room and she sat and talked awhile with the other ladies in the home. We went to the dining room and sat down at a table and talked to the caregivers. Everything was agreed on—until the time of the move.

The Final Moments at Mother's Home

"I'm not going to leave my house...I'm not going to leave my garden," Mother insisted constantly. She locked herself in her bedroom, fell on the bed and began to weep. Her crying could be heard throughout the entire house, and through the open windows in the houses on either side. She kept saying, "I don't want to go...I want to stay here."

"Mother, don't cry," I pled. "There's no alternative. We have to make this move." I spelled out all the options again. We had no other choice. Then she reiterated all her arguments. "Get Laurine...Get Mrs. Barnes..." Alzheimer's victims are like that. They forget what they have said, so they say it again and again and again.

Petite Erin Towns was stubborn, and as strong as the giant oak that grew outside the back door. I have never seen a man or a woman stand up to her. Right was always right, and she was the defender of right as well as its gatekeeper. Mother had always been right, and confident she was right. I never saw her weak side. I was 61 years old and had never seen my mother cry. Here she was lying on the bed crying. She created a scene that went on for an hour.

After we were finally able to take her to Green Acres Home, I talked with my brother and sister. We all said the same thing: None of us had ever seen her cry. She had been too strong for tears. Then it dawned on me. She was crying, but there were no tears. I asked my brother and sister whether they noticed she shed no tears when she cried. Yes, they both noticed. I wondered if she did not know how to cry so she did not realize there should be tears. Had she been so strong all her life that she never learned how to cry? On the other hand, she could have been faking it. If so, she was doing a bad job because her eyes were not wet and the tears had not come.

Finally Martha said, "That's enough, Mother. We must go." Martha took her by the hand and did something she had never done in her life: Martha was firm with Mother.

Mother got up, we walked out the front door and locked it. When she got to the car, she stopped and said, "I've got to feed my dog."

"I'll do it," I told her, and I went back to the house and into the kitchen. I took the cold grits off the stove and mixed dry dog food with the rest of the fried chicken left over from our meal. I put it on a plate and set it on the back porch for her dog, named Tiger.

Then a strange thing happened. Tiger would not eat. He stared at me, and I saw in the dog's eyes something I had never seen in my mother's eyes. Tiger had tears in his eyes. Tiger seemed to understand what was happening. Did he know he would not see Erin Towns again?

I will never forget the eyes of that dog...shedding tears.

Part I

Teachers

Our greatest teachers light a fire in our souls that burn a lifetime. They motivate us to learn more, reach higher and reach beyond the captivity of our circumstances. They relive their own dreams through the accomplishments of their students who believe their lessons and aspire to their vision.

Jimmy Breland showed me the strong thread that ran through the *whole* Bible. He gave me a love for the Scriptures and for the heroes who changed history. He instilled in me a hatred for cigarettes and alcohol. I am a teacher because of him.

Margaret Logan motivated me to rise above insurmountable obstacles. She believed in me. She introduced me to a new world within the cover of books and gave me an appetite to read—everything. Her teaching style motivated me to write term papers. I am a writer because of her.

"Jimmy Breland taught the __Whole__ Bible"

1

Jimmy Breland: Why I Love Sunday School

A tall, thin man from Walterboro, South Carolina, came to Savannah, Georgia, during the Depression looking for a job. The only work he could find was selling coffee door-to-door for the Jewel Tea Company.

One morning when I was about five years old, Jimmy Breland knocked on the door at 107 Wagner Street to pitch his wares to the lady of the house—my mother. I was standing beside her as she sat in an old wicker rocking chair covered with chipped, dark-brown paint. I watched as she selected several packages from the wooden sample tray Jimmy Breland had placed on the floor. I was fascinated by this coffee salesman's bony Adam's apple protruding from his long neck. Thick, black, chest hairs stuck out from under the collar of his frayed white shirt.

As he got up to leave, Jimmy Breland looked right into my eyes. "Y'wanna go to my Sunday School?" he asked, enthusiasm penetrating through his Southern drawl.

"Yes, sir!" I responded with all the excitement of a preschooler. I would probably have gone anywhere with him.

Jimmy Breland bubbled with enthusiasm as he told about telling stories, singing songs and coloring pictures of Jesus. Then he added, "We have a sand table where we'll make paths over hills, just like where Jesus walked!" He walked his two fingers over an imaginary hill, the way two fingers in the television commercial walk through *The Yellow Pages*.

"Wow!" I exhaled with wide-eyed response. "Mama doesn't let me put sand on our table." I was ready to go with him to Sunday School that very moment. I turned to Mother sitting in the wicker rocking chair and blurted, "Can I go?"

"What church do you attend?" Erin Towns asked, looking for a reason her son could not go to Sunday School with this salesman. She did not want me going to some strange church. If she had known what a cult was in those days she would have been doubly concerned. Maybe she also feared that my going to Sunday School would interfere with the lifestyle she and my daddy were enjoying at the time.

"Eastern Heights Presbyterian Church," Jimmy Breland said.

"Presbyterian," echoed my mother. That seemed to answer her objection because she herself had been brought up and married in a Presbyterian church in South Carolina. My mother did not give up easily, and when she did not want to do something it took an explosion to change her mind. She thought for a moment, then spoke.

"But that church is on the other side of town," she objected. This young mother was still looking for reasons not to get involved or not to send me to Sunday School.

"See that black truck?" Jimmy Breland said, pointing through the screen door out to his truck in the street. "I'll come get him in that black truck." Looking at me he said reassuringly, "I'll pick you up every Sunday and take you to Sunday School."

My mind was fixed on the big black truck showing gold letters that spelled "Jewel Tea and Coffee Company." I had seen the truck on many occasions, and what kid does not like to ride in a truck? It looked to me as though Jimmy Breland's answer should have convinced my mother to let me go with him, but she was not ready to give up.

"But little Elmer doesn't even attend regular school," she object-

---

Sometimes an adult will make a promise to a child, then forget to follow through— often crushing the child's dreams. [But Jimmy Breland did not forget.]

---

ed again. She said she knew where the church was located, and that it was surrounded by fields. She said she was afraid I might wander away from the church and get lost in the nearby ditches. To my mother that ended the conversation.

But Jimmy Breland said, "I'll pick him up when he goes to public school in September." He gave me a wink.

Finally Erin Towns nodded her approval. "But not until September," she reminded the coffee salesman.

There was a certain finality in my mother's statement. Whenever Mother spoke there was a sense of finality. Around the Towns's household, her pronouncements were law. I followed the tall man outside to his truck and checked the corrugated boxes as he placed his tray in the back. There didn't seem to be enough room for a little boy among all the boxes.

"I'll come get you when you go to school," Breland promised as he left.

A Promise Is Kept

Sometimes an adult will make a promise to child, then forget to follow through—often crushing the child's dreams. The next time Jimmy Breland, the coffee salesman, returned to sell us some more coffee, he seemingly failed to remember the little boy staring up at him with wide eyes. While he talked about coffee with my mother, I dreamed of riding in the back of his panel truck.

He forgot, I thought as I followed him quietly to the front porch.

"Don't forget." Breland jerked around, looked down at me and announced, "You're going with me to Sunday School when you get to the first grade."

In September, 1938, I started attending the first grade at Waters Avenue Public School. True to his word, Jimmy Breland told Mother he was coming to take Elmer Towns to Sunday School. A soft misty rain covered the bushes and lawn. Puddles of water covered the dirt street where I lived. The sky was not dark or threatening, though; it was a bright day and the sun was trying to break through the rain.

Jimmy Breland's black panel truck glistened as it came splashing through the mud puddles on Wagner Street. I was waiting on the front porch, dressed in white short pants and filled with anticipation. I was ready. I had no way of knowing that the experience would change my life. Seeing the truck, I dashed down the stairs.

"Come back!" Mother yelled. "You'll get wet!" She told me to wait until Jimmy Breland pulled up to the house.

When he did, he waved to us. "Ready to go?" he called cheerfully.

I would have gone with him anywhere.

He went to the back of the panel truck and opened the door. I wondered where I would sit. I had previously peeked into the back at the stack of boxes, and it seemed to have no room for a little guy. On that wet, Sunday morning when Jimmy opened the back door, however, I noticed the back of the truck was empty.

Every Saturday evening Jimmy Breland carried the Jewel Tea boxes into his living room so his truck could carry children to Sunday School.

"Smells good in here," I said as I jumped in and inhaled the aroma of ground coffee.

From Wagner Street, Breland drove to Helmkim Street to pick up the four Aimar boys. Then it was on to a nearby housing project to pick up several more boys and girls. Eventually it was a two-mile trip down the dirt road that later would be called Cedar Street and on to the church. The church was a two-story red brick building set on a low hill, the highest point in Savannah. It was only 53 feet above sea level, but in flat Chatham County it was appropriately called "Eastern Heights."

Eastern Heights Presbyterian Church

Eastern Heights Presbyterian Church averaged about 100 in Sunday School in those days, just as it did 12 years later when I left for college. The plaster walls of the auditorium were painted a stuffy yellowish color. The knotty-pine floors were covered with several coats of aging varnish.

Mr. Frank Perry, the general Sunday School Superintendent, faithfully led what they called "opening exercises." His wife played the piano as the entire Sunday School, from small children to elderly women, sang three hymns. Those who had observed birthdays during the previous week were encouraged to come forward and drop coins—one for each year of their lives—into a Heinz 57 Varieties pickle jar. No matter how old, everyone brought pennies and dropped them—*thunk, plink*—through a slot in the lid of the jar.

At the end of opening exercises, the entire Sunday School stood to sing "Onward Christian Soldiers." Then everyone marched in procession to the classrooms. The Beginners sitting on the second row (no one sat on the front row) marched into the center aisle, then to the back of the auditorium, and on to their Sunday School class. The Primary class followed the Beginners because they were the next oldest. After them followed the Juniors, next the Intermediates and then the High School class. The adults remained in the auditorium for their class. This ritual made a young boy appreciate growth and advancement. When I marched with the smallest kids, I was already looking forward to marching with the older kids.

Hitting the Jackpot

Jimmy Breland usually remained for the preaching service after Sunday School so my father picked me up after Sunday School. Only we got home much later. Father always stopped for a drink or two before going home. Once we spent our Sunday afternoon at Barbee's Pavilion, a dance hall built over the Isle of Hope River. Daddy gave me several pennies to play the slot machines. One of the coins hit the jackpot, and 127 pennies poured out of the slot machine onto the bar, off the bar under the bar stool and out onto the dance floor.

"Look—the kid hit the jackpot!" someone said. Some of the dancers stopped and began to help me pick up pennies. A drunk crawled around under the bar stools looking for pennies. As they handed me pennies, I stuffed my pockets with my newfound fortune. The pennies, however, were so heavy that my pants began to slip down. Fortunately, a barmaid came to the rescue; she used a safety pin to attach my pants to my shirt, then another one to fasten the pockets shut so the pennies would not spill out. When I finally arrived home, so proud of my winnings, Mother yelled at Daddy for taking me to such a place after Sunday School. The yelling went on for a long while.

Caring Makes a Difference

Jimmy Breland faithfully took me to Sunday School. I don't know whether I would have gone without his influence. Although Mother attended Sunday School as a girl, and had been married in that little country Presbyterian church, she had not attended church regularly when she moved to Savannah. She and Daddy had lived on the wild side.

Jimmy Breland made a difference. He took me to Sunday School, and cared for me spiritually. Although he did not lead me to Christ, he gave me a foundation for my salvation.

Principles to Take Away

1. *The shepherd principle.* Jimmy Breland taught me the importance of doing more than imparting knowledge to students. He showed me by example to care for the total needs of the students I would have later in life. I learned that a good Sunday School teacher is a shepherd.
2. *The reproducing principle.* I also learned that good teachers reproduce themselves in the lives of their students. They live beyond their own limitations and reproduce in their learners their own dreams and values.
3. *The principle of developing potential.* Jimmy Breland taught me the importance of developing the potential of each student. No student was unimportant to him. The fact that

many of Jimmy Breland's learners became teachers shows how his investment in them paid off.

4. *The inscrutable-interactive principle.* The student gives life back to the teacher who breathes his spirit into his students. They are bound together in the inscrutable bond called "teaching."

"Wanting to go to Sunday School at age five"

2

The Water Pitcher: Learning the WHOLE BIBLE

The Kitchen Sunday School Class

Finally the day came when I was promoted to the Junior Department in the Sunday School of Eastern Heights Presbyterian Church, and Jimmy Breland was my teacher. I felt big when I marched out of the auditorium with the "older" juniors. No longer would I march with the little children. At the singing of "Onward Christian Soldiers," I joined 24 other youngsters marching upstairs to the church kitchen, where Jimmy Breland's class met.

That kitchen just might have been the best classroom ever. Great teachers do not need great facilities. They do not need great teaching aids, or great equipment. Jimmy Breland brought energy into the classroom, creating a great learning environment. His was one of the greatest classes I ever experienced.

The typical tall-ceilinged kitchen was grimy, showing years of accumulated grease. A massive black cookstove that seemed as large as an army tank was parked against one wall. It was greasy to the touch. Under the window was a dingy-gray galvanized sink, deep enough to allow for stacks of dishes. A large food-preparation table with a stainless steel top stood in the center of the kitchen. It was perpetually wiped clean by the fastidious ladies of the church. Above the food-preparation table hung utensils, suspended from the ceiling on hooks, ready to help in preparing food. Hanging from the hooks were pots, knives, frying pans of various sizes, big forks, long-handled spoons and any other tool that did not fit into a drawer.

The kitchen was big—too big for just cooking, but large enough for lots of kids. So the kids sat in adult-size, wooden folding chairs on one side of the food preparation table. Jimmy Breland taught from the other side, walking from one end of the room to the other so he could look around the hanging utensils. Good teachers keep eye contact with all students, and Jimmy Breland could always see every pair of eyes. No one could hide behind a large pot.

Jimmy Breland called us scalawags, and we lived up to his pronouncement. The wooden slats pinched when we rocked the chairs, and frequently someone yelled out "owee!" Then we all laughed. Because the chairs were meant for grown-ups, our feet did not reach the floor. So I pulled both feet up on the chair seat and wrapped my arms around my knees. When a girl tried it, someone giggled and said, "I see your panties!" The usual fidgeting occurred, but Jimmy Breland was a great teacher. He maintained discipline and we learned.

The room was also characterized by a large, square hole in the wall, through which food could be passed during church dinners. By 1940 standards, the kitchen was as modern as money could buy, and it was a source of pride for the members of Eastern Heights Presbyterian Church. On Sunday mornings, however, that church kitchen was the launching pad for the world's greatest Sunday School teacher—at least he was the greatest for two dozen juniors.

Jimmy Breland stood behind the antiseptic food counter gazing into the eager faces of boys sitting to his left, girls to the right. Isn't it ironic that girls, who usually had the right answers, also sat to the right? The boys crowded to the left, not wanting to be touched by a girl. Sometimes it seemed that Jimmy Breland could look into our very gizzards, the innermost being of a boy.

Teaching the WHOLE BIBLE

The first Sunday I was in his class he hunkered down over the stainless steel table and announced, "I'm gonna teach you the WHOLE BIBLE."

Wow! I responded inwardly. *The WHOLE BIBLE!*

The Bible was a mysterious black book I saw in our home and in the home of all my aunts and uncles. People spoke with reverence about the Bible. "Don't ever put anything on top of a Bible," I was told.

Mischievous little boys who got into devilment from time to time were scalawags; and I was a scalawag, just like Abraham.

Now here Jimmy Breland was saying, "I'm gonna teach you the WHOLE BIBLE from cover to cover."

Some critics today might cringe at the idea of any Bible teacher making such a claim, especially someone like Jimmy Breland who had only an eighth-grade education. But Breland could excite young minds. He could electrify dreams; and he taught his juniors "the WHOLE BIBLE."

Breland did not lecture. He did not give speeches. When he opened his mouth, enthusiasm flowed. It would have been obvious even to a casual observer that he was excited about what he knew. He was a storyteller, and his junior boys and girls stepped into the world of his story. He didn't just tell stories about Abraham; he made Abraham live. When he told how Abraham obeyed God, I wanted to obey God. When he told about Abraham's lie about his wife Sarah, the class cringed with guilt.

Breland was not schooled in the use of Greek, Hebrew or biblical exegesis, but he was remarkably fluent in the language generally understood by kids growing up in Savannah, Georgia.

Abraham, Who Began It All

"Abraham was a scalawag!" Breland declared. People in my hometown knew that a scalawag was a mischievous boy dabbling in devilment. A scalawag was not an evil boy, but an average boy who liked to tease and play, and who didn't always obey. Mischievous little boys who got into devilment from time to time were scalawags; and I was a scalawag, just like Abraham.

When Breland caught someone not paying attention, he reached up among the utensils above his head and grabbed an old aluminum water pitcher. He didn't have the sort of visual aids publishers provide for Sunday School teachers today, so he used a water pitcher.

"This pitcher is Abraham, who began it all," he announced, holding up the dented pitcher.

Twenty-four pairs of eyes focused on that dented pitcher. He waved it high above our eyes, and everyone kept watching. "This is Abraham, who began it all."

Maybe because he was a Presbyterian, Jimmy Breland always described Abraham as the one "who began it all." He was no doubt aware that Adam was the first man, so in a way, of course, Adam began it all. To some "Covenant Presbyterians," however, the covenant of grace is dated from God's covenant with Abraham.

"Who is the water pitcher?" Jimmy asked a boy not paying attention. He always focused on students not focused on him.

"Abraham," the boy answered. That wasn't the answer Jimmy wanted from the student. Jimmy wanted a complete answer.

"Abraham, who began it all," Jimmy Breland added. "God poured His grace into Abraham." The effect was captivating as he walked over to the sink and filled the pitcher with water. "God poured His grace into Abraham so Abraham could be emptied onto the world."

Even the greatest Sunday School teachers in the world have moments when they encounter difficulty captivating the attention of every pupil. Whenever Jimmy Breland lost our attention, he did what good teachers always do to regain it. He asked a question.

"Who is the water pitcher?" he asked, waving the pitcher in front of the boy whose thoughts had begun to wander.

"Uh...uh...," the boy stammered. "The water pitcher who began it all."

The answer was close enough to win a smile from Jimmy Breland as he corrected, "*Abraham*, who began it all."

The next week in Sunday School was more of the same. Jimmy Breland began the class by holding up the water pitcher and asking, "Who is this?"

"Abraham, who began it all," the class cried in unison.

"Aw, you can do better than that," Breland coaxed. And better we did as we hollered, "ABRAHAM, WHO BEGAN IT ALL."

The Sins of the Fathers

"This is Isaac," Breland continued, as he reached for the sugar bowl. "This week's lesson is about the son of Abraham."

That day the class heard the story of Isaac's birth to the 100-year-old "Abraham, who began it all." Whenever he lost eye contact with his students, Jimmy Breland rescued it with a question. "Who is the water pitcher?" Sometimes he asked, "Who is the sugar bowl?"

The next week he added, "Who are the salt and pepper shakers?" He held them high as he walked back and forth in front of the class. The salt and pepper shakers, we learned, were Jacob and Esau respectively, the sons of Isaac. Breland explained how Abraham lied, next Isaac lied, but the biggest liar of them all was Jacob. From behind the food preparation counter in the kitchen of Eastern Heights Presbyterian Church, this master teacher soberly announced, "The sins of the father are passed on to the son."

The thought terrified me. The greatest sin of my father was drunkenness—at least that is what I thought was the greatest sin. The senior Towns was a good man who loved his children, but alcohol was beginning to destroy his life. He was not just a closet drunk. Everyone in the neighborhood had seen him staggering home. I could remember the times I had been sent out into the street to help my drunken father get up from the dirt street and lumber into the house. Neighbors sat on their porches laughing at the man floundering in the dirt. I was embarrassed, and I cried as I helped my drunken father home. Then when we finally got into the house, my mother's yelling could be heard several houses away.

Of course I did not want the sins of my father passed along to me. So I reasoned in Sunday School class: *I don't want to be a drunk like my father.* Perhaps there in the kitchen of Eastern Heights Presbyterian Church where Jimmy Breland taught about the sins of the fathers is where I determined never to take my first drink of whiskey. This commitment was strictly kept for the rest of my life.

Review Time

"Let's review," Breland said each week. He began the class by holding up the various utensils from the kitchen. There was the water pitcher, the sugar bowl, salt and pepper shakers, a butcher knife, the knife sharpener, the potato peeler and even a Coca-Cola glass. The list seemed as endless as the Old Testament itself. We always took great delight in helping Jimmy Breland remember the utensils he forgot.

Occasionally he teased us. He held up the meat cleaver for the 400 years in Egypt, but we all knew it represented the 400 years of the Judges—the knife sharpener represented the 400 years in Egypt.

Nonetheless, Breland taught us "the WHOLE BIBLE." He included the prophets such as Obadiah, Micah and Zephaniah, putting them in their proper chronological sequence among the kings. We learned what each prophet did and how he fit into the historic sequence of God's plan. Week by week, the faded yellow walls of the kitchen in the Eastern Heights Presbyterian Church witnessed an odyssey of supernatural proportions.

Lives were being changed.

I remember the day Jimmy Breland began the class with a review that started with Abraham and marched through all the Old Testament books. He lined up the kitchen utensils on the edge of the stainless steel table, one after the other. We kids shouted out the biblical character as Jimmy Breland held up a utensil. The butcher knife divided the kingdom of Solomon into the tribes of Israel to the north and Judah to the south. Some in the class could repeat from memory the kings of Judah. Then we came to the postexilic books—Ezra, Nehemiah and Esther. We covered those, too. And that was the end of the Old Testament.

Job, as in "Robe"

"Do you know who this is?" Jimmy Breland asked, holding up a Coca-Cola glass.

"No," we said in unison, shaking our heads.

"The Coca-Cola glass is the next book in the Bible," Jimmy Breland said, smiling. We began to thumb intently throughout the Old Testament to find the book that followed Esther. I found it, but didn't call out.

"Elmer?" Breland said, seeing that I had found the place in my Bible. "Who is the Coca-Cola glass?"

"Job," I said, pronouncing the name like a working "job" a person is paid to do.

"No it's *Job*," Jimmy Breland corrected me, pronouncing the *o* as in "robe."

I did not want to be disrespectful, but I had to come back with, "Looks like Job to me," again pronouncing it like "job."

The best Bible survey I have ever had of the <u>*Whole Bible*</u> *was with Jimmy Breland, who started his class with a dented water pitcher and "Abraham, who began it all."*

The class laughed. Jimmy Breland ignored me and took the Coca-Cola glass and asked dramatically, "Where does Job fit on the table?"

We shook our heads back and forth, for we didn't know. Jimmy Breland held up the Coke glass over the kings and said, "He doesn't go here." Then he held Job over the times of the Judges and noted, "Doesn't go here." He walked slowly, dramatically, quietly down the line of kitchen utensils and finally put the glass next to the water pitcher and announced, "Job and Abraham were contemporaries."

I didn't know what that meant, and I'm not sure anyone else in the room knew. Jimmy must have sensed our frustration, for he then said, "If Job and Abraham were little boys, they would have played together." We all understood that.

That survey of the Old Testament has stuck with me through the years. I have taught a Historical Survey of the Old Testament to university students and written a textbook about the topic. The best Bible survey I have ever had of the WHOLE BIBLE, however, was with Jimmy Breland, who started his class with a dented water pitcher and "Abraham, who began it all."

Lessons About Smoking and Drinking

In the third grade several of us were standing with Jimmy Breland in front of Eastern Heights Presbyterian Church when he spied a church member tapping a Lucky Strike cigarette on a pack, as a smoker will do just before lighting up.

"Don't ever smoke your first cigarette," Jimmy announced to us with authoritarian finality.

"Why not?" a young male voice asked.

"It's dumb," was Jimmy Breland's retort. "You waste a lot of money when you smoke cigarettes," he said. He did not moralize or give a more Christian reason. Jimmy Breland did not smoke, because he was tight with money. He bragged about never buying a car. Instead, he always looked for a job driving a truck for someone else so he could avoid making payments or buying gas or insurance. So as a youth, I went to Sunday School with Jimmy Breland in a truck belonging to Jewel Tea, one belonging to Atlantic Richfield, a linoleum truck and a venetian blind truck. When Jimmy was killed in an accident while driving a truck delivering linoleum, he had still never bought a car.

Jimmy Breland never bought a house either. He told us not to purchase houses because we might lose them in the next great depression he was sure was coming. He lived in a garage apartment, then in a housing project, and told us, "You pay only $13 a month to rent in the projects and they cut your grass."

So because Jimmy was cheap he told the boys in his class not to smoke. It was simply a waste of money. As we stood in front of the church he turned to me and said, "Would you like to burn up a dollar bill?" Obviously, I shook my head no. Then he added, "You might as well gather grass off the lawn and roll your own cigarette in a dollar bill and burn up the money."

Because of Jimmy Breland's exhortation, I never had my first cigarette (see chapter 21, when I almost smoked). My mother smoked when I was young. She came from a family of 11 children and all my uncles on her side of the family smoked; but I didn't, because of

Jimmy Breland. My daddy came from a family of nine children. He smoked, and all his brothers except Uncle Herman smoked; but I never smoked, because of Jimmy Breland.

A few weeks later the same boys were standing in the same spot in front of the church with Jimmy Breland. He pointed to two men standing on the other side of the flower bed and sidewalk.

"Those men can't be elders in this church because they drink," he said. We all knew Jimmy Breland was talking about liquor. Then Jimmy told us, "Don't ever take your first drink of liquor." Again, he didn't appeal to moral or religious reasons. "Drinking liquor is like pouring a bottle of money down the commode." He gestured dramatically to illustrate holding a liquor bottle over a commode.

"Do you like to flush away money?" He asked the question of the impromptu class of boys. We all shook our heads negatively. "Then don't take your first drink of liquor!" he said matter-of-factly.

My mother drank when I was small. All my uncles from my mother's side were hard-liquor-drinking dirt farmers in South Carolina; but I never drank, because of Jimmy Breland. My father was a helpless addict to alcohol and went to his grave, never beating his addiction. All my uncles from my daddy's side were alcoholics except Uncle Herman. But Jimmy Breland built in me a desire to break the addiction. I never took my first drink of whiskey.

Communicating Lasting Lessons

According to an early count, 19 of the 24 of us children in Jimmy Breland's class went into Christian ministry. Dr. Albert Freundt became the distinguished professor of church history at Reformed Presbyterian Seminary in Jackson, Mississippi. Others became pastors, missionaries and Christian school teachers, and I became a college president.

Once I was having lunch with Dr. Frank Perry, another product of Jimmy Breland's class, who grew up to be pastor of a 1,400-member Southern Baptist church on the north side of Atlanta. Knowing of my love for college teaching, he asked, "Who was the greatest teacher you ever had?"

I suspected the question was not straightforward, and he had an ulterior motive. "What are you getting at?" I asked. Dr. Perry told me he was trying to determine why so many of us from Eastern Heights Presbyterian Church went into full-time Christian service.

"Jimmy Breland," I replied immediately.

Then Dr. Perry looked at me and asked, "Who was the spatula?" We laughed as friends do when they know the answer to a question that bonds them together.

Jimmy Breland's love of the Bible became my love. He communicated passion and dreams. He made God's Word live. He had very little to work with, just average boys and girls from average homes. His classroom was not conducive to teaching and contained no educational furniture or equipment. He had an eighth-grade education. Yet his teaching electrified his students and I learned the WHOLE BIBLE.

Principles to Take Away

1. *The passion principle*. The greatest teachers have an unquenchable love for their subject matter. They do more than communicate facts; they generate a love affair between student and lesson.
2. *The principle of salt-on-the-tongue*. Great teaching is not just giving answers for quizzes. A teacher sprinkles salt on a student's tongue and points to water. I learned that motivation is the indispensable ingredient in teaching.
3. *The glue principle*. Teaching is more than giving facts to be learned. Jimmy Breland showed me that I learn best when I gain an insight that glues facts together.
4. *The practical principle*. Sometimes a good practical reason for not engaging in harmful practices such as smoking and drinking rings truer than trying to theologize about it.

"Seventh grade inspired me—1945"

3

Miss Logan: Someone Who Liked Me

Entering Seventh Grade

My seventh-grade teacher was Margaret Logan, an attractive young lady in her late 20s. Later in life I saw a snapshot of her and thought she looked like the typical girl next door. If she had gone to the right beautician who could do her hair properly, she could have been Miss Savannah or Miss Georgia. She was tall, a little thin, and had an infectious smile.

When I walked into room 107 at Chatham Junior High School,

however, I did not see an attractive lady. I saw an old, old teacher. Like an old board fence that needed painting, or the old barn in the middle of the field, Miss Logan was not attractive to me, because I did not like school or anyone who was attached to school.

"So you're Elmer Towns," Miss Logan said as she greeted her new student. "I want you to know I've heard all about you," she continued.

That figures, I thought to myself. I had always been suspicious that teachers had it in for me. Seventh grade would be no better. The

---

Miss Logan believed in dreams.

More importantly, she convinced her students

they could do anything they dreamed.

---

teacher had as good as confessed her complicity, and the class had not even begun yet. Yes, it was going to be another long and difficult year.

"But," she quickly added, "I don't believe a word of it."

"Uh...yes ma'am," was all I could say at the time.

A little confused, I made my way to my usual place in school—the back rows of the room, a place I now affectionately describe as "the lunatic fringe." Actually, my placement in the back of the room was because my last name was Towns more than anything else. In most cases, class seating charts were arranged by the teacher based on an alphabetical order of last names. That meant *A*s at the front and *T*s toward the back. By the time I was in a situation where I could choose my own seat, I was in the habit of sitting in the back rows.

I began to think that maybe, just maybe, seventh grade might be different. There was something about this new teacher, Miss Logan. Somehow she seemed different from the rest. In the weeks to come, I learned more fully what that something was. Miss Logan believed in dreams. More importantly, she convinced her students they could do anything they dreamed. The result was dramatic. I went from failing the sixth grade to being on the honor roll in the seventh.

Miss Logan sat at a small, white, oak desk at the front of the room, near the windows. Behind her were large blackboards—not the green boards that later came into use, or the white boards on which we use felt markers today. These were deep black, and when I wanted to irritate a girl I could scratch my fingernails across them and produce that marvelous, screeching E-E-E-E-E sound. The greatest satisfaction of scratching fingernails across a blackboard is not fraying nerves, but the screech of girls who yell, "Stop!" or put their hands over their ears.

Chatham Junior High School had at one time been the Savannah High School. In 1932 when a new high school building was created on the south side of town, the old building became the junior high school. The stone arch over the main entrance bore the date 1903 chiseled in stone. But in the seventh grade you don't notice dates chiseled in stone.

What I did notice when I walked into the building was the wooden floor. The hardwood floor looked like the decks off a sailing ship. Perhaps they were so old that they could have come over on the *Mayflower*. I wore a brand-new pair of penny loafers with hard leather heels, and I could make them sound *rat-a-tap, rat-a-tap* as though I were doing a well-synchronized tap dance. I enjoyed walking the halls of Chatham Junior High School.

Room 107 had the tall ceilings that were customary in the early part of the 1900s. Because there was no air-conditioning, tall ceilings made the rooms tolerable on hot days. High on the walls were hung the portraits of three pious-looking presidents, the portraits that traditionally hung in American school rooms—Washington, Jefferson and Lincoln. Perhaps some educator thought they might motivate us to "Go and do likewise."

The World of Books

Within a few weeks after the fall school term began, Miss Logan immersed her students into a whole new world—the world of books. One morning she marched her class single file along the hall to the winding wooden staircase at the rear of the building. The wooden stairs were known as the "up" stairs. We followed her up the "up" stairs to the third floor, then through the third-floor halls to the library. At the door to the library was a wide, steel staircase that went straight down to room 107. These, as you can guess, were the "down" stairs. The school had a rule that children could only walk down the steel stairs and up the wooden stairs.

That kind of rule was a challenge to a boy like me. Later that term, after first checking to make sure everything was clear, I ran up the "down" steel stairs just to see what would happen. I heard no lightning strike or loud claps of thunder, not even the flapping of an angel's wing. Triumphantly, I looked both ways on the third floor, and marched back down the conquered "down" steel stairs to the first floor.

Miss Logan, however, kept the rules, so her class had taken the long way to the library. That day, the students remained in the library with their teacher for three periods. Miss Logan sat on the small stool students normally use to reach books on the high shelves. She spread her full skirt around the stool, then gathered her students around her on the carpet. We all sat on the floor, and I was folding my arms around my knees. She began that day by reading poetry. I listened. I did not think I would like poetry, but I liked what I heard. I liked Miss Logan, too.

My Passion for Biographies

Before our visit to the library ended, Miss Logan offered another experience for me. Near the tall windows was a separate bookcase marked *B*. The teacher explained that the *B* stood for "biographies," or stories about people.

"I want everyone to check out a book on your hero," Miss Logan announced. "At the beginning of each day, someone will tell the class about the hero."

Having taken my usual place at the back of the group of students sitting around Miss Logan, I was one of the last to reach the biography shelf. By the time I arrived, the books about Washington, Jefferson and Lincoln had been snatched. All that was left on the shelf when I got there—or at least that I cared to read—was a biography of Lou Gehrig, first baseman for the New York Yankees. That night I took home the book about Lou Gehrig.

"I read the WHOLE book!" I told Miss Logan excitedly after I returned to school the next morning. As near as I can remember today, that was the first book I had ever read cover to cover. Triumphantly, I walked up the wooden "up" stairs to the library to return Lou Gehrig, then walked down the steel "down" stairs carrying another biography under my arms. I was hooked. I had discovered the world of books. For several weeks I took biographies home and read them, usually in a single night. The next day I advised Miss Logan again of my progress, announcing, "I read the WHOLE book!"

"Who will volunteer to work in the library stacking books during recess?" Miss Logan asked one day. Miraculously, the boy who had never volunteered for any academic project and had attended school for six years eagerly awaiting the recess bell raised his hand. For the remainder of the school year, I carried a pint of milk and the four sandwiches my mother had prepared to the library where I ate my lunch and stacked books. Most of the time not many books needed stacking, so I sat and read another biography. "Another WHOLE book!" Miss Logan responded when I boasted to her of my accomplishment.

Checking the Appearance Chart

In addition to teaching English, history and social studies, Miss Logan was also my homeroom teacher. That meant she conducted the class assembly each morning. Together the class sang the national anthem, and pledged our allegiance to the flag bearing 48 stars and hanging in the corner of the room. Then Miss Logan selected a boy to read a psalm. "You read like a minister," she often commented when other boys read. Somehow she never seemed to say that about my reading.

Opening exercises concluded each day by checking the appearance chart. As each child stood at attention next to his or her desk, Miss Logan announced, "Inspection time." Seeking the help of one of the prettier girls in the class, she checked appearances. Name by name she went through the list, checking off various categories. Eventually she came toward the end of the list and called the name "Elmer Towns."

Quickly I snapped to attention as the chosen cute little girl came by to inspect me. "Fingernails," Miss Logan announced. She believed everyone should have clean fingernails. I held out all 10 fingers for the cute girl to inspect. Before entering class each morning, the boys in room 107 stood outside digging underneath their nails with a penknife to be sure they got a check on Miss Logan's chart.

"Shoes."

"Check." The pretty inspector responded. Only a few days into the fall term, I had advised my mother about needed changes to my wardrobe.

"We can't wear sneakers because they won't polish," I announced. In seventh grade I polished my shoes regularly, even when it wasn't Saturday night. If they got dusty on the way to school, I was proficient at polishing the left shoe with the back of the right trouser leg, then reversing the order.

"Check," the cute girl echoed. Another mark for Miss Logan's chart.

I had also told my mother, "Miss Logan says we can't wear T-shirts to school because they don't have a collar." Mother simply shook her head in unbelief and secret admiration of the teacher who could transform the clothing habits of her 13-year-old son.

Among the items on Miss Logan's checklist were teeth. "Elmer," my mother declared in amazement one morning. "You're brushing your teeth."

"Yes, ma'am, Miss Logan...," I mumbled through the foaming Pepsodent.

Mother understood.

Helping the War Effort

Miss Logan motivated her class with dreams. She believed the members of her class could do whatever they dreamed possible, regardless of the obstacles. In 1944, involvement of the United States in World War II meant cutting back on government spending at home.

"There's a war on and we can't get money to paint our room," Miss Logan announced one day.

The class decided we would do it ourselves, no doubt having Miss Logan's encouragement. None of us had painted a school classroom before, but we knew we could do it and do it well. We collected money for the paint and, sure enough, we did the job ourselves, not even using a borrowed ladder.

My part in the project was painting the ceiling. By placing a small table on top of a larger table, I was able to reach the ceiling by climbing on top of this unique scaffold. Up near the ceiling of room 107, I felt important. It was more than just a sense of pride because my buddies were watching, or fulfillment that comes from doing a job well, or even pleasing Miss Logan. It just felt good to be looking down on those three stern, presidential faces that had been looking down on me all year.

The eternal optimist, Miss Logan sought to motivate us on to perfection. "We must help win the war," she pled one day. "We can help defeat the enemy if we place a Red Cross poster in every store window in Savannah."

The eternal optimist, Miss Logan sought to motivate us on to perfection. "We must help win the war," she pled one day. "We can help defeat the enemy if we place a Red Cross poster in every store window in Savannah."

"Every store window in the WHOLE town?" I asked.

"Every store that has a display window must have a poster," she explained. The need for blood was great, and the class that met in room 107 wanted to do its part for the war effort.

Miss Logan divided Savannah into several sections and assigned various students to place a Red Cross poster in every store window in that section. I was assigned the west side of downtown Savannah, an area littered with bars and pawn shops, the kind of place seventh-grade boys probably should not frequent. But I went there anyway.

"But ya gotta have one," I pled with a bartender who refused the Red Cross poster. Leaning over the bar on his hairy arms, the man looked down at the boy with the overenthusiastic, seventh-grade approach.

"Why?" he asked disgustedly.

"Because it will help win the war," was my sincere response. I was as certain I was doing my part to win the war as surely as if I had been fighting on some forgotten island in the Pacific or bombing some important military target in Europe.

"Okay. You put it up," the bartender consented.

I put the poster in the window and felt a sense of accomplishment. I was helping to win the war; I was accepted in the class as an equal; but most important of all, I was accepted by Miss Margaret Logan.

Motivating Students with Love and Acceptance

Young boys can be motivated to action in many ways. Some adults yell at them, some beat them and some use guilt. All these means of motivation have different degrees of effectiveness in getting the job done and internally influencing boys on their way to manhood. Many of these methods, however, cause a boy to become a belligerent man.

Miss Logan motivated with love and acceptance. She made me want to do a job and to be a better person. She had a positive way of making me believe in myself.

She was the first teacher I really tried to please. She dramatically changed my attitude toward school, especially toward reading books and, as the next chapter reveals, writing term papers.

Principles to Take Away

1. *The freedom principle.* Miss Logan gave me "permission" to grow, to explore and to journey beyond her expectations and beyond the experience of the other students. I grew in the freedom of Miss Logan's class.
2. *The principle of unexpected acceptance.* I never expected a teacher to accept me, much less to like me. At age 93, Margaret Logan thought back on 1944 and said, "I liked Elmer Towns and I think he liked me."
3. *The journeying-within principle.* I had to journey within before I could journey without. Margaret Logan helped me find myself, find out who I was and find out what I could do. Internal self-discovery always runs hand-in-hand with external self-development.

"Miss Logan taught me to dream—12 years old"

4

The Term Paper: Learning to Write

Researching a Term Paper

Miss Logan helped me express myself by helping me with my writing. Before I entered her class, I only wrote what was required of me. When she expressed surprise and excitement about my first term paper, it motivated me to write more.

She took us to the library often. Her love of books became our passion. One day in the fall of 1944 when she led the class up the wooden "up" stairs of the library, she announced, "Everyone is going to write a paper that will be seven pages long." She took her place on the small stool. We gathered around her on the floor. She spread her full skirt around her legs and promised, "I'll help you."

Although seven pages sounded like a big term paper, I had no doubt in my mind that I could do it. If Miss Logan thought I could write a seven-page paper, I knew it could be done.

"Everyone choose a topic for your term paper," she urged as she passed out slips of paper. I took a slip from the bottom of the pile and passed the others on to the next student. Slowly I unfolded the topic slip and read the three words printed on it: *The Panama Canal.*

What could I write about the Panama Canal? I wondered. Almost immediately, my buddies began comparing topics. When I saw the topics chosen by my friends, I was disappointed not to be writing about a war or some great hero.

Ugh...who cares about the Panama Canal? I concluded.

Miss Logan began to teach us that day how to research a term paper. She took us across the library to the reference section to show us how to use an encyclopedia. She looked at one boy's paper to see his topic, then reached for the appropriate volume of the encyclopedia and began to read aloud. She showed the class members how an encyclopedia article could help them write their term papers.

From the encyclopedia she took us to a dark oak cabinet she called the "card catalog." Miss Logan told an amazing story of how an Englishman named Dewey thought up the Dewey Decimal System while listening to a sermon. She further explained that the system divided all knowledge into tenths, and that the larger division number was a survey of the whole. The first tenth of each division was always a topical introduction no matter how small the division. (The lecture made such a great influence on me that years later I wrote a book about how to begin and organize a Sunday School library, in which I used the Dewey Decimal System. See Elmer Towns and Cyril Barber, *Successful Church Libraries* [Grand Rapids, Mich.: Baker Book House, 1967]).

After explaining how to use the card catalogue that day, Miss Logan had each student look up his or her topic. I found seven 3x5-inch cards describing seven books about the Panama Canal. When it was time to return to our regular classroom, I went to the shelf and checked out all seven books. I also checked the encyclopedia to see if it contained information about the Panama Canal.

The term paper became longer and longer every time I read

another book about the Panama Canal. I read the encyclopedia articles, looked up the geography in an atlas and read a history book about how men dug the ditch from the Atlantic to the Pacific. In the process of my research, I found an article that sketched a side profile of the canal showing the height of each lock and the gallons of water it took to lift the ships from lock to lock. The final paper was seven pages long and had an appendix that included a scale profile drawing of the canal. I traced the profile on onion skin paper, and added it to my term paper.

The Panama Canal Speech

After the paper had been turned in, Miss Logan stopped me as I was leaving for recess carrying my milk and sandwiches.

"After recess, will you give a report to the class on the Panama Canal?" she asked.

I agreed and headed off to the library. Not until I reached the door of the library did a brainstorm hit me. Hurriedly, I ran down

---

"Elmer...," Miss Logan paused for words.

"That speech was wonderful!" What could a boy say?

"Shucks," was the best I could say.

---

the steel "down" stairs and returned to room 107. Miss Logan had already left. Using a yardstick, I covered the blackboard with a wide-scale profile of the canal similar to the one on the onion skin paper. The scale drawing was completed as the recess bell rang. The sketch of the Panama Canal stretched from one end of the blackboard to the other. Miss Logan seemed impressed because she immediately called on me to give my report. I walked to the blackboard and simply told the story of how many cubic feet of dirt were moved in each section, how the ships were lifted, how far the saltwater tide went inland and the size of the mountain that had to be cleared for the canal to be completed.

"Elmer...," Miss Logan paused for words. "That speech was wonderful! I've learned more about the Panama Canal from you than I've ever known before."

What could a boy say? I shuffled my feet, and my ears turned red as I flushed with embarrassment. I couldn't look her in the eyes. I had wanted to do a good job, but Miss Logan seemed to think it was even better than she expected.

"Shucks," was the best I could say.

The Headiness of Praise

As soon as the class period ended, I rushed up the wooden "up" stairs to the library hearing the words of Miss Logan echoing in my mind. Quickly I looked up the name "Suez Canal" in the encyclopedia and began the process again. More than anything else, I wanted to hear those words of praise again.

Miss Logan was shocked when I turned in an extra report about the Suez Canal several days later. "That's wonderful, Elmer," she said. One of the great disappointments of this second research was to learn that the Suez Canal had no locks. Miss Logan had apparently not noticed the length of the report, so I drew it to her attention.

"It's 14 pages, twice as long as the other paper."

"That's wonderful," she said again. And it must have been so. It included several misspelled words, but the paper rated a 98. I kept waiting for Miss Logan to ask me to present an oral report about the Suez Canal. I hung back in the class at recess, giving her the opportunity to ask me. Seventh-grade boys, however, don't get everything they want in life, and I did not get to present a report about the Suez Canal to the class.

The History–Paper Challenge

The following spring, Miss Logan again took the class to the library. This time she had another assortment of paper slips containing term-paper topics.

"This term paper is for history," she said. She was again sitting on that little stool with her full skirt spread out. The class sat on the rug surrounding her. "Your last term paper was for a grade in social studies, but this paper will probably be longer."

Miss Logan gave the stack of topics to a girl who began the process of handing out topics. Each of us took a slip of paper and passed the others on as before. Some were not sure they could depend on the slip on the top to be acceptable, so they took theirs from the bottom of the stack. When it came my turn, I closed my eyes and took the slip of paper at the bottom of the stack. Passing the other topics along to a classmate, I turned my slip over and read, "A History of the Wars between China and Japan."

"Wow!" I exclaimed. "This paper will be LONG."

Some of my friends were not so sure I had a good topic, but I was ecstatic. Perhaps the constant news of the war in the Pacific had heightened my interest in the Orient. At that point, however, I think any topic would have excited me. This was a challenge.

Preparing a New Place to Study

To prepare for what I suspected would be a gigantic undertaking, I decided I needed a special place to study. Our two-bedroom home at 107 Wagner Street was too crowded to afford privacy, or even a

---

I had a dream, and a dream can help even an average person achieve a goal against insurmountable odds.

---

desk, so I usually studied on the kitchen table or the dining room table. I always had to put my stuff away at mealtimes, though, so I decided to renovate the neglected garage and use it for a study.

The garage was little more than a place for junk to collect and spiders to spin their webs. Its wood was rotten, it leaked and one side was bent out of shape by tree roots growing under the foundation. The oil-packed, black dirt floor made the place smell more like a transmission shop than a library. The building should have been torn down, but it was to become the study of Elmer Towns, seventh-grade researcher. I had a dream, and a dream can help even an average person achieve a goal against insurmountable odds.

Holding a can of tar in hand, I began patching the leaky roof. I was not concerned about covering the whole roof, only that section over the area where I planned to study. Next I nailed an old wooden apple crate to the wall, which became a bookshelf. Beside the bookshelf, I placed a table I had nailed together with two-by-fours and some other old lumber. I covered the table with a piece of old linoleum to make the top smooth enough for writing. Because I had made the desk too high, I had to return the chair I had borrowed from the dining room and sit on a barrel. Even then I had to place the barrel on a box to sit high enough for my elbows to reach the table.

On a visit to the library, I had checked out two armloads of books and brought them home in an old army knapsack. Placing the books neatly on my apple-crate bookshelf, I stood back to view my new study. I was pleased. Everything looked perfect. What more could I want? "After supper," I said, "I'll come out to begin working on my term paper."

True to my determination, I hurried out to the garage after supper to begin work on the paper. That is when I noticed my slight miscalculation. The garage was pitch black. The garage had no electricity, so of course my study was in total darkness. My youthful plans had not included lights. My zeal collapsed.

Every dream has its temporary setbacks, and that was all this problem was destined to be. I knew I could solve it. Womacks, the local grocery store, sold six-foot extension cords for nine cents each, as I remember. Using my mother's yardstick, I measured the distance from the back-porch light to the desk. Later, having bought more than a dollar's worth of extension cords, I plugged them one into another and stretched the line from the porch, down a fence, and through the pomegranate tree until a light socket with a naked light bulb hung just over my desk. Then with renewed conviction, I began to write.

The Influence of a History Project

Miss Logan, you ain't seen nothing yet, I thought as I read of various Sino-Japanese conflicts and included them in the paper. And I was right. After several weeks of diligent reading and writing, the paper became longer and longer just as daylight in the spring days was also lengthening. By the time I finished the project, the sun was still shining after supper and the garage was light enough so that the naked light bulb was only marginally helpful.

I produced a 99-page term paper entitled, "A History of the Wars

Between China and Japan." Naturally, the margins were wide and my handwriting large, just as a seventh grader would normally make them. For me, writing a 99-page paper broke mental barriers. I did something I thought I would never do, and I did it at a younger age than I expected. A 99-page term paper built self-esteem. If I could do that, I could write a book. My mother kept that paper for years.

Can anyone measure the full influence of a seventh-grade teacher four decades later? Miss Logan taught me to dream. Years later, I was able to become a college president, and later to begin the new college of my dreams. Writing a paper about the history of China and Japan created a deep love for the Orient that has resulted in several trips to the Far East both as a political commentator and a religious leader. Having convinced myself I could write a book, throughout my teaching career whenever I was unable to find an adequate textbook for a particular course, I wrote one.

Principles to Take Away

1. *The breaking-the-barriers principle.* I wrote more for Miss Logan than for any other teacher, breaking through all barriers, because I knew she would like it and affirm me for doing it. Young people can break their mental chains if we support them.
2. *The love-finds-a-way principle.* Because Miss Logan loved me, I found a way to exceed her expectations. I would have done anything for Miss Logan.
3. *The affirmation-motivation principle.* Miss Logan demonstrated that children will work much harder and longer for someone who praises them than for someone who criticizes them.

Part II

·—··—··—··—··—··—··—··—··—·

Mother

Mothers exercise the greatest influences on our self-perception because we are the extension of their dreams, values and prejudices. A mother usually expects her children to become more than she became and accomplish more than she achieved.

My mother taught me: You're a Towns—you can do anything you want to do. But in some ways I think she expected me to do what *she* wanted to do, but could not.

Mother taught me to be on time and never to give in to the weaknesses of the body. She said that a strong will can make the body do almost anything. She made me believe that the average person can rise above circumstances even with limited resources and in difficult circumstances, and get the job done.

"Erin Towns should have been Dr. Towns"

5

Erin's Pride: Sewing Up a Pigeon

When I was 13 years old, I built a pigeon coop and began racing pigeons with the men of the local Racing Pigeon Association. I won only a single race; it was with a young bird that had flown into my coop bearing a leg band from Mississippi, more than 500 miles away. (Once a band is placed on the pigeon, the band can't be removed without cutting off the bird's leg.) Every time I released my pigeons for a practice race, this Mississippi pigeon always came back first; it would not return to Mississippi. One day my mother saved the pigeon's life. Here is how it happened.

Mother Sews Up My Pigeon

One thing a pigeon owner never does is let the birds eat wet corn. Wet grain will swell up in their gullets and choke them. The expanded grain won't digest, and the birds can't eat anything else. They die of starvation. One night I put out too much grain, and the pigeons did not eat it all. The grain became wet overnight and when my prize pigeon from Mississippi ate it, her gullet swelled beyond belief.

"She's gonna die," I yelled, and ran into the house to tell Mother. We took the bird to the dining room table and I held it on the back.

Using the sterilized needle and plain black sewing thread, Mother stitched the bird's neck back together. "Just like darning a sock," she said.

Mother examined the gullet. First, she tried to get tweezers down the bird's throat to remove the grain.

"You'll kill her," I protested.

"She'll die anyway," Mother said.

The tweezers did not work. Next, Mother tried to put an eyedropper down the pigeon's throat and with reverse action suck out the wet corn. That did not work either.

"We'll operate," Mother said. "I'll slit her throat with a razor blade and sew it up," she said matter-of-factly.

"She'll die," I said again.

"She'll die anyway."

Mother told me to get a needle and sterilize it over a flame, then do the same thing with a razor blade. She plucked the feathers from the pigeon's neck and washed it with alcohol. Our dining room table became an operating room.

"You're not a veterinarian," I protested.

"I've seen a horse doctor do this," she replied. "Horse doctor" was her term for a veterinarian. "They can sew up a mule, cow or horse—why can't I sew up a pigeon?"

I shook my head in disbelief. I had seen my mother pull the neck off a chicken for frying, and I thought she was doing the same to my favorite pigeon.

"We're Townses," she said calmly. "We can do anything we want to do."

With a single incision, she sliced the neck from the head to the breast. It only took one swipe. The bird flayed, but I held the wings steady. My young eyes saw Mother thrust in her fingers and pick out the swollen corn. Using a ball of cotton she cleaned out the inside of the gullet. I looked inside my pigeon, thinking it would be filled with blood, but I saw only a small amount. Then, using the sterilized needle and plain black sewing thread—we did not have white thread—Mother stitched the bird's neck back together.

"Just like darning a sock," she said.

The pigeon lived, and I called her "Erin's Pride," for my mother. Amazingly, the bird flew again after having its throat cut. After the operation Erin's Pride won the 500-mile race from Gulf Port, Mississippi, to Savannah, Georgia. It was also amazing that it returned to Savannah from its original home in Mississippi.

Mother Sews Up My Cousin

A couple of years later, I saw my mother sew up one of my cousins, either Paul David O'Cain or Carl O'Cain. I don't remember which. We were playing pirates on the picket fence at my grandfather's home in Sardinia, South Carolina. I did not see the accident. I was walking on the top of the fence when my cousin fell and slit the inside of his thigh on the sharp wooden point of the fence slat.

I was attacking another ship or dueling with buccaneers (probably outdueling them) when I heard my cousin yell in a way I knew meant danger. He went running for the kitchen holding his leg. I don't remember how they sewed my cousin back together. He was stretched out on grandmother's bed, yelling a blue note. The rest of the kids were corralled up on the front porch. We were scared.

The emergency room of the hospital in Sumter, South Carolina, was 22 miles away. Although that's no distance at all today, it seemed an insurmountable barrier when I was a kid. We only went to Sumter once a week and that was on Saturday, and everyone piled into one car.

I had experienced many cuts in my life, and I knew my cousin was in serious shape. Mother pulled the flesh together with a Band-Aid after washing the wound with iodine or peroxide. "But a Band-Aid or adhesive tape won't hold this cut together," I heard her say to the other ladies in the bedroom. There was concern about the length of the wound. "If it breaks open, it won't heal."

"Also, it'll get infected," someone told my mother.

"I'll just sew him up," Mother said. "Hold him still," we could hear Mother command her helpers.

"I don't want to sew his peepee to his leg." That's what my mother called the penis. We heard her, and laughed. Then we looked at the girls and got embarrassed.

Today the whole scene may seem laughable, but back then sewing up a boy's leg in the bedroom was frightening. Isn't that the way it is with a lot of things? They are not quite as serious as we think at the time.

Aunt Leila, my cousin's mother, was not there. If she had been, she would not have let her sister Erin stick a needle into her son and sew him back together. She was not there, though, so Mother stitched him up. He was crying the whole time.

"Why didn't you take him to the hospital?" Leila yelled at Mother when she got home.

"There was no car..."

"Why didn't you send Elmer to run to a neighbor's?"

"We sewed up the animals when we were young," my mother yelled back.

"My son is not an animal!" Aunt Leila had a hot temper.

The argument never ended. Mother and Leila were born two years apart and were the best of friends—but like many friends they argued vigorously.

Mother always maintained she did the best thing, given the times and culture. She stood at the hinge of medical progress. She knew of neighbors who died of infections from simple cuts and accidents around the farm. She grew up without penicillin, antibiotics and other miracle drugs that became available in her later life. She did what was necessary, whether sewing up a cousin's leg, pulling teeth with pliers from the tool shed, or administering a mixture of turpentine and castor oil to cure a stomachache.

Those were different days with different attitudes. Few people consider sewing up a leg today. We are scared silly of being sued for malpractice or child abuse. We are afraid infection could set in and the leg might have to be amputated. In the rural areas of yesterday, however, often no car was available to run to the hospital and no doctors were located nearby. Mother was worried about my cousin bleeding to death, and about scarring and infection. In her determi-

---

In Mother's determination, she knotted up the black thread as if finishing up a hem on a dress, and said, "Pour in iodine to kill any infection." My cousin screamed, but he lived.

---

nation, however, she knotted up the black thread as if finishing up a hem on a dress, and said, "Pour in iodine to kill any infection." My cousin screamed, but he lived.

The McFaddin History Stone

Mother was born into the McFaddin family and taught me McFaddin history. I knew very little about the history of the Towns family. I don't know if it was because Mother and Father argued so much that she hated the Towns family, or because she did not know Towns history, but never—not once—did we visit my father's birthplace, Social Circle, Georgia. Yet once or twice every year we visited Sardinia, South Carolina, to visit Mother's birthplace. When we went in the early summer, we stayed all summer.

"Let's go to the cemetery," Mother said every time we visited Sardinia. Technically, the cemetery was in Gables, the neighboring "wide spot" in the road. They were not really towns, but just wide spots in the road. The area was named by the U.S. Post Office located in a general store at each place.

Although she did not tell us the Towns history, Mother said, "A Towns can do anything." I knew when she took us to the cemetery that she would stand us in front of the gravestone and tell us again, "A Towns can do anything you want to do." I knew the speech was coming, and I looked forward to it.

The McFaddin cemetery was located on the banks of the Black River, but the river actually looked like a swamp. For hundreds of yards, on either side of the meandering Black River a thick undergrowth of cypress trees with their spreading roots were visible. A variety of other trees formed a canopy high overhead. The ground around the cemetery was tabletop flat, so just a small rain forced the river out of its banks. It formed a gigantic mud flat where bushes, vines and underbrush seemed as thick as the Amazon rain forest—at least to me as a young kid. To many people a swamp is ugly and threatening. To most people from South Carolina, however, a swamp is beautiful.

The McFaddin cemetery was lined with a cattle fence. A grass-covered trail went straight through the middle of the tombstones. It led us past family names such as DuBose, Melton and Missap; but most of the markers read "McFaddin."

Right next to my grandfather's grave was the McFaddin History Stone. It was a gigantic, gray granite stone that stood eight or nine feet tall—to a little kid it was as big as a house. It told how John McFaddin settled the area in 1728, before the city of Savannah was settled. History books call them the eight land-grant families of the Carolinas. These eight families were each given land grants to a different river and the land for miles on each side of the river.

"The Black River was given to the McFaddins," my mother told us as we stood in front of the McFaddin History Stone. "You're special."

It was almost like a queen telling her son, the future king, that he would have the kingdom and that he was special. Mother had me stand in front of the McFaddin History Stone and reminded me that McFaddin blood ran in my veins.

"I expect more of you," she asserted, and I felt I had a divine mandate to reach higher than the average kid, to be better than the average kid, to accomplish more than the average kid.

A Towns Can Do Anything

"Remember who you are—you're a Towns," Mother said, speaking toward the gray granite stone in the cemetery. And I heard what she said. Educators call these events "teachable moments," and standing in front of the McFaddin History Stone was one of those events for an impressionable youth.

One thing I do not understand to this day. Mother was proud to be a McFaddin, and to her dying day she never tired of telling me about McFaddin history. Why then did she tell me constantly, "Remember—you're a Towns"?

Maybe it was just the heritage she was giving me, not necessarily a specific name. Maybe she had identified with her last name, and she was bonding me to her and her background. "You're a Towns, you can do anything you want to do!"

Mother did not have much money, but she could feed and clothe us. She could stitch up a pigeon and a cousin and make them live. Mother taught me "You can do what you want to do" because she did it first.

Principles to Take Away

1. *The self-respect principle.* I learned that the Towns name was important, and that I was expected to live up to its standard. When I did it, I gained self-respect and felt I was important, too.
2. *The principle of give-it-a-shot.* I learned that it is important to hit your obstacles head-on. I learned not to give up without at least trying.
3. *The principle of necessity.* I learned that in life you can do what you have to do. I learned that you can stuff your feelings into your pocket and do what you can to try to save a pigeon's life.

"The whole family pulled together"

6

The Born-Again Piano: Making Do

We had a "born-again" piano in our house that was life changing.

My sister, Martha, wanted to take piano lessons, but we did not have money to buy a piano. Mother and Dad talked about it, when they talked—but that was not often. Whenever Martha went to visit Aunt Ina's, she headed straight to the piano. Aunt Ina had an old-fashioned, round-topped piano stool that went higher when spun counterclockwise, and lower with a twist of the wrist clockwise. Martha spinned the stool as high as it could go and still remained steady. Her dangling legs far removed from the foot pedals, she played simple music "by ear." Someone pointed out to her where the notes in the hymnbook were on the keyboard, and she learned to play simple pieces even without lessons.

"She's got to have lessons," Mother said to my father. "If she can play that well without lessons, what could she do...?" Her voice trailed off.

"We can afford it—go ahead," Daddy said.

"We don't have a piano," Mother said logically.

That is where Aunt Ina's piano comes in. After Uncle Marion died, Aunt Ina divided her two-story house and rented out the

We talked about fixing everything, because "A Towns can do anything." I never had a doubt we could repair the pile of junk.

downstairs. The piano was too big to move up the twisting stairs from the living room, so it was left in the downstairs hall for a couple of years. Then, by neglect, the piano was stored on the back porch. Only a screen protected it from rain, so the wood veneer peeled, the oak cracked, the metal strings rusted and some of them broke. The piano was a mess.

"Send the truck from White's Hardware to pick it up and bring it home," Mother told Daddy.

"The piano doesn't work," he complained.

"It'll do for practice, even if it sounds bad," Mother insisted.

I had learned "You can do anything you put your mind to," so I met the delivery man from Daddy's store at Aunt Ina's. We moved the piano to the living room of 107 Wagner Street.

Martha sat down to play, but about half the keys did not work. We took off all the boards and stripped the piano down to the frame holding the giant, heavy steel sounding board that stretched the strings. We made a list of everything that was missing. We needed 10 or 12 strings, some felt to absorb the hammers, five or six hammers, seven or eight ivory key coverings, several small wooden rods that connected the keys to the hammers as well as other items.

Three of us—Mother, Martha and I—spread out the guts of the piano over the living room rug. We talked about fixing everything, because "A Towns can do anything." I never had a doubt we could repair the pile of junk.

"Daddy can get wire at White's Hardware for strings," someone said.

"I'll cut strips of felt from one of my old hats to absorb the hammers," Mother offered, getting excited.

"We can glue the felt with my model airplane glue," I added.

"We can cut up my jewelry box for keys," Mother said. She owned a cheap, white plastic jewelry box. We cut it up into pieces shaped like piano keys and glued them in place with model airplane glue. The cheap white plastic shone brighter than had the yellowed genuine ivory.

"I'll get dowels from the planing mill," I said, because my daddy's hardware store didn't sell lumber. I used my model airplane knives to cut the dowels to size.

"Let's sandpaper this ugly cracked paint and give it a nice mahogany finish," Mother suggested. So we removed the paint with paint remover and filled in the cracks with wood putty. I cut small pieces of wood at my junior high shop class to fill in the broken boards or places where the veneer had peeled. After we put it together, it looked new. Well, almost new. But the sound was worse than the tinny plinking of an old rag-time piano in a B Western movie.

"We need to tune it," Mother said. We did not have money to pay a tuner, or we were too embarrassed to have one look inside our makeshift job. I found a skate key and it fit the bolts that held the piano wire at the end intended for tuning.

"I can't turn the key," I told Mother. The next day I took the key to the bicycle shop and had a long steel rod welded to the key. This handmade key was strong enough to turn the bolts and adjust the sound. Martha could now play the scale.

"Do, he (not re—it was a sour note), mi (another sour note), fa, sol, la, ti, do." We played the scale again and again until we got each note to sound right in relation to the note below it and above it. If a note sounded like a step up from the previous sound, we left it alone. Eventually, we got all the keys to stair step the sound from the lowest to the highest.

Martha learned to play on that makeshift "born-again" piano.

Daddy paid for the lessons, and when Martha went to college, she was pianist for the college chorale.

Principles to Take Away

1. *The dominant-will principle.* My mother taught me I could do anything I wanted to do. What makes this principle work is *choice.* If I chose to do it, I could get it done. Of course this does not mean I am omnipotent. I choose not to do a lot of things I know are impossible, and things I don't care about.
2. *The "make–do" principle.* When you don't have all the resources, "use what is usable." Some may put it, "There's more than one way to skin a cat." I say there are many ways to get a job done. I have to find the way that works best.
3. *The principle of creative innovation.* I think of all the children who did not learn to play the piano because they did not have one. Because it was important for my sister to play the piano, we all pitched in to make it happen. It was not a good piano—not even a second-rate piano. It was barely adequate, but with a little creativity it did the job.

"We learned joy in simple delights"

7

Cans and Cake: We Ate Better than Did the Rich

When you do not have much money, you do what you need to do to get food. We always had a garden for vegetables, and usually had chickens for meat and eggs. We always had one or two hams around the house.

Canning Butter Beans

"We're going to work in the cannery today," Mother announced. I then planned to work all day canning vegetables.

The cannery was next to the high school in Gable, South

Carolina, a small school having fewer than 60 high school students. The cannery was nothing but a shed with a roof, and screen wire to keep out the insects. Inside the shed were five large tables on which the vegetables were prepared.

"Erin, which table is yours?" asked Mr. Milsap, who brought in several baskets of ripe tomatoes. All the farmers wanted Mother to can their vegetables because she did the best job. The school provided the tin cans and the steam to cook the tomatoes, so a third of the canned vegetables went to the hot-lunch program for school kids. Another third of the vegetables went to Mother for her labor, and the other third went to the farmer who grew them.

"I've got enough tomatoes," Mother told Mr. Milsap. "I need butter beans or snap beans."

"I've got 'em at home," he said, climbing into his pickup truck to go get what Mother wanted. Another lady took the tomatoes for her day's work.

When I unloaded the bushel baskets of butter beans (Yankees call them lima beans), I knew what my day's work would be. For a couple of hours I shelled the beans. My mother, sister and I, along with our cousins, sat in a circle under the shade of a grove of small oak trees. Shelling beans was necessary if we wanted to eat, so we knew better than to complain. Steady work in the hot summer meant good hot food in the winter.

The beans were cooked in a large pressure cooker, which readied them in a short time.

After operating the machine to seal lids on the cans, I had to test them in water. Mother always warned me that if I messed up one can, we could all die of botulism.

Using a black marker I wrote on the top of each can the letters "BB." Everyone knew it meant butter beans. We had prepared only 13 cans of butter beans. If we had canned tomatoes, we would have had 50 or 60 cans. We got a lot more cans of tomatoes for the same work because they are much bigger than butter beans.

"But butter beans taste better," Mother said, explaining why fewer cans were better. Then she said, "Four cans for us," as I put them in the car. "And four for Mr. Milsap," she said, as I put them on his shelf. "And five cans for the school."

I was quick to determine that dividing 13 cans into three shares left one extra can. "Why don't we take the extra can?" I asked. "No one will know."

"We'll do what's right," Mother explained. "Because *we'll* know what we did." When Mother spoke, we did not debate. I knew how to answer:

"Yes'm."

That day we canned butter beans, snap beans and a few cans of okra. When Mother was planning our workdays in the cannery, she was also planning our fall meal schedule.

Although some children are afraid of ghosts or bogeymen under their beds, that was never my problem. The space under my bed was filled with butter beans.

The cans were taken home to be stored under the beds. We had only three closets in our small house, and they were for clothes. So I always had cans of vegetables under my bed. Although some children are afraid of ghosts or bogeymen under their beds, that was never my problem. The space under my bed was filled with butter beans.

"We eat better than rich people," Mother always told us when she was cooking dinner. She pointed to a simmering pot and said, "Butter beans are better when we can them ourselves."

"Yes'm."

"They're better with a little fat from our chickens."

"Yes'm."

As a kid, I absolutely knew my mother was the best cook in the world. I loved her cooking. I ate the cooking of my aunts and the moms of my buddies in the Cat Patrol. Not a mother compared with mine. Mother constantly told me, "We couldn't eat better if we had all the money in the world."

Although we were poor, I always had plenty to eat, and we had well-balanced meals. We always had root vegetables and green vegetables, usually four or five on the table at each meal. What was not eaten was put in the ice box. It was reheated for the next meal.

"Let Them Eat Cake"

Marie Antoinette, the vicious queen of King Louis XVI who influenced the French Revolution, was told that the poor had nothing to eat. She said, "Let them eat cake." The queen must have known Erin Towns. Because after we ate a nutritious, well-balanced meal of vegetables and meat, we had cake for dessert. Never pie. Always cake, or milk and custard. And it was homemade cake, not store-bought cake, even if it was made from a mix instead of from scratch.

I don't remember seeing my mother roll out a pie crust with a rolling pin, or trim the crust of a pie. Maybe it is because we did not have money. Maybe she did not like pie.

K-rations were dry, yucky and bland.

I bought a K-ration one time for a nickel,

and wished I had bought two candy bars.

"Elmer," she told me, "go get some cake mixes from the Army-Navy Store."

I went to the mantel above the stove and selected three or four pennies. Then I peddled my bicycle about a mile to Pennsylvania Avenue to the Army-Navy Store. It was a messy place best described by its clutter. Gigantic piles of surplus goods were stored everywhere, stacked without rhyme or reason. The aisles were narrow, the floor was dirty and I waded through waste paper like surf on a beach.

The Army-Navy Store had been a roller rink until the boys left for World War II military service. The girls did not want to skate alone, and the owner could not make money off children who were left behind, so he converted his roller rink into an Army-Navy Store. He sold a lot of olive green army clothing and leftover military junk, stuff the Army and Navy did not want.

I knew exactly what I wanted when I arrived at the converted roller rink. I locked my bike to a chain-link fence and headed to the rear right corner where two lumbering stacks of cartons were placed. The first stack contained K-rations, the food soldiers ate in the field when an army mess could not cook a hot meal for them. K-rations were dry, yucky and bland. I bought a K-ration one time for a nickel, and wished I had bought two candy bars. During World War II, candy bars were usually a nickel apiece if you could find them. You could buy two stale Hershey bars for a nickel at the Army-Navy Store

Next to the K-rations was placed a tall stack of cake mixes. The boxes were olive green—what else? They were ugly boxes because the manufacturers dipped them in wax—I suppose to keep them dry when an army truck sloshed through a swamp or the cook tent was drenched by rain. I could barely read through the heavy wax coating. The only words printed on the boxes were "white" or "yellow," designating the flavor of the cake mix inside.

The cake mixes were about the size of a pocket Dictaphone or a bar of soap. That is not a lot of cake, but a soldier could pour the cake mix in his battle helmet liner, add water and cook cake for dessert over an open fire. I imagine it was a delicacy to a cold soldier who had just finished a cold meal of K-rations.

These cake-mix boxes the size of a bar of soap contained enough powdered flour to rise with heat—I said they "swelled up" to about twice their original size. So from one of these boxes of cake mix Mother baked a cake about twice the size of a bar of soap.

"Take a nickel," mother told me, "get five boxes." The cake mix was a penny a box. Mother added eggs because we were fortunate to have chickens in the backyard. That made our cakes rich. Then she added milk instead of water. She baked the batter in a square cake pan and cut the steaming hot cake into squares.

She never iced them with chocolate or vanilla icing. I guess a box of icing cost too much. But a nickel's worth of army cake lasted almost a week.

"My Favorite Pie Is Cake"

My wife has seen me pass by the pies at a church supper and cut a large piece of cake instead. When I get back to my table where no one can see me, I take a spoon or fork and scrape off the icing. Then I sit back and take a big bite of warm cake—plain cake, simple cake. Simplicity is the story of my life.

Once my wife and I were playing games at a church party. We were up front as contestants in the game, "Do You Trust Your Wife?" The wife is sent out of the room and the husband is asked to make decisions about certain issues. Then the wife is brought in to face the group and is asked the same question they asked of her husband.

While my wife was out of the room, they asked me a simple

question: "What is your favorite pie?" I had trouble with the question, so they clarified it. "When you order pie for dessert, what kind do you order?"

Of course I was having trouble with the question because I do not order pie. If it is served at a banquet or church supper, I eat it; so it is not that I do not like pie. It is just not my first choice. If given the choice, I choose cake.

The people playing the game were impatient. They chided me, "Come on...give us an answer."

So I told them simply, "My favorite pie is cake." Everyone laughed and I laughed with them. But when I am given the choice, I will choose cake.

My wife returned to the room and they asked her, "What is your husband's favorite pie?"

She thought about it for a few seconds. She remembered that I usually "pass" on the pie. Without having discussed my own answer with me, she answered with a quizzical smile, "Cake. His favorite pie is cake."

Principles to Take Away

1. *The planning principle.* Because my mother planned what to can in the summer, we always had well-balanced meals on the table in the winter, and had more than enough to eat. She planted her garden in monthly stages so we would have fresh vegetables all summer.

2. *The enjoyment principle.* I learned the importance of enjoying what you eat, and eating what you enjoy. Both come by choice. I learned to enjoy cake both because it was all we had and because I made a choice to like it. We would be much happier in life if we made up our minds to enjoy what we have.

3. *The "vanilla" principle of simple delight.* Some find happiness in exotic things, but I have found incomparable delight in the simple things of life. I say profundity is found in simplicity. We tire easily of gimmicks, yet never fully appreciate the enduring goodness of vanilla ice cream and plain cake.

Part III

-- -- -- -- -- -- -- -- -- --

Friends

Our childhood friends help us cut the psychological umbilical cord that has made us see ourselves through our parents' eyes. Our friends overlook our faults because they are not responsible for us. They show their approval by their acceptance. Their encouragement helps us to become adventurous individuals.

I learned that I enjoyed doing things with my buddies of which my mother disapproved. I learned about a good life beyond her domain. My friends taught me to be a person my mother could not control. I saw my "transgressions" through their eyes, which was different from what I saw through Mother's eyes. Sometimes my friends controlled me; at other times I walked away to become my own person.

"I sneaked and was caught"

8

The Water Tank: Is Sneaking Fun?

"Let's go swim in the tank!" someone said one hot July day.

Savannah can be insufferably hot in July, the temperature reaching over 100 degrees and the humidity as high as the temperature. I was one of seven or eight boys in Wagner Heights, the part of town we lived in. We called ourselves the Cat Patrol. The Cat Patrol usually ran around barefoot and wore short pants in the summertime. Our knees and ankles were usually black with dirt and our short hair was uncombed, although most of us had flattop haircuts so we did not need our hair combed.

"We're not supposed to swim in the tank," someone cautioned.

There was always the danger that Mr. Mixon, David Mixon's father and the superintendent of the cemetery, would catch us swimming in the water tank. We were wisely afraid of him. We heard he beat his son with a belt, and we were all afraid it might happen to us if he caught us in the tank.

The water tank was a large, wooden water tower in David Mixon's backyard and belonged to Hill Crest Cemetery. Water was pumped out of the ground and stored in the tank for watering the cemetery lawn. The tank also supplied water to the inhabitants of Wagner Heights. The five streets of Wagner Heights were technically in the city of Savannah, and sometime around 1944 we got city water. Before that, we paid Hill Crest Cemetery 50 cents a month for water.

We were quite a sight. Six or seven naked little bodies lying flat on a wooden platform, all looking straight up at the sun.

Obviously, little boys who had dirty knees and black feet should not swim in the water supply of Wagner Heights, but on occasion we did.

"We'll wash off first," someone reasoned. So we all decided to wash, and then go swim in the water tank. The process was dangerous, but on some days it was so sweltering hot that the risk was worth it. We went in pairs or one by one to the back of David Mixon's house, not wanting his mother to see us all appear in the backyard at once. If she did, we knew she would tell Mr. Mixon.

Boyhood Misadventures

So on this day we sneaked one at a time into the backyard, took the hose that hung on the back of the Mixons' house and washed thoroughly, then climbed up a wooden ladder to a flat wooden platform about as high as the roof of a house. When we got to the platform, we lay flat so no one could see us, and dried off in the hot sun. Lying there on the platform, we waited for other members of the Cat Patrol to arrive. Arriving in David Mixon's backyard, they gave the secret whistle, and we whistled back the "all clear" signal.

We were quite a sight. Six or seven naked little bodies lying flat on a wooden platform, all looking straight up at the sun. The July sun is so bright in Georgia that we squinted. It pierced our eyes like a white-hot needle.

Our swimming pool was a large, round, wooden tank like those used on cattle farms in those days to water the herd. The wooden beams were held together by several steel bands. Perching on its homemade water tower, it looked like a large coffee cup poised above the ground on white-painted wooden poles on which the paint had badly faded over the years.

The water was about 8 to 10 feet deep. A constant flow of clear artesian water entered the tank, but green algae or moss always floated on the surface. Obviously, the water tank had no top.

"Yuck! We drink this stuff?" I said to the gang.

Unconcerned About Unsanitary Water

As I look back at that water tank, it did not seem unsanitary in the early '40s. At my grandpa's place, we hauled water in a bucket out of an artesian well at the foot of the stairs. He did not have running water in his kitchen. Sometimes, when the well went dry, we had to walk half a mile to the "branch" (our word for the stream that ran through his farm) to get a bucket of water for the house. The water from the branch was cloudy, so we let the bucket sit for a while so the sand could settle to the bottom of the bucket.

Because I drank the sandy water at the branch at Grandpa's house, I did not think that drinking water from Hill Crest Cemetery's water tower was that bad. After all, the green slime floated on the top of the water, and the pipe to Wagner Heights emptied out from the bottom of the tower. We all knew that water from the subterranean depths of Savannah was safe, so we had no concern.

"I'll beat you with a belt," Mr. Mixon told us one time when he caught several of us on the platform getting ready to go into the tank.

"I will not tell your Mother," he warned. "I'll beat you myself."

We believed him. He had told us we could not even go onto the water tower platform, much less swim in the tank.

Swimming in the Forbidden Water Tank

The day we decided to swim in the water tank, Mr. Mixon was out on the other side of the cemetery, cutting grass. We had checked his whereabouts before going up the tower. We also checked to see how much grass he had left to mow. We did not want him coming home early and finding us in the water tank.

When no one was watching, we quickly climbed the last 10 feet on a metal ladder and slid over the edge, dropping into the tank. Fresh water from the artesian well poured continuously into the tank through a two-inch pipe. We swam under the water flow, and we swung off the pipe.

"Don't pee in the water!" we told one another. After all, we were civilized and we would eventually have to drink that stuff. I can honestly say I never did pee in the water, but I am not sure about some of the other guys in the Cat Patrol.

"Cool, man...cool," we said. We never stayed long in the tank because we had nothing to hang onto except the ladder and the two-inch pipe. It was not much fun having six or seven boys hanging onto the same ladder. We jumped into the water, swam out and dog paddled back when we got tired. Sometimes we swam off from the water pipe, but not too often. We could be seen from the neighborhood when we swung on the pipe.

When we had swum long enough, we slipped out of the tank one by one to lie flat on the platform again so no one could see us. There, naked before God and the blistering Georgia sun, we dried off and swapped stories. It only took about 15 minutes to get dry. Then again, one by one we sneaked down the wooden ladder into David Mixon's backyard. Like bank robbers with devious motivations, we walked away in different directions.

Before the great escape, however, we decided where we planned to meet to continue our play. After playing for the rest of the day, at least two or three hours, I thought I had pulled off another one. I had gone swimming in the forbidden water tank, and got away with it.

Mother Knows Best

"Hi, Mom," I said as I pushed open the front screen door. She was sitting at the dining room table and I saw a switch on the table in front of her. She did not smile. She did not speak. She just stared at me. "Where did you play today?"

"Around."

"Is that all you want to say?"

"Yes'm."

"You've been swimming in the water tank."

"No ma'am. Not me," I stuttered and stammered. "It was Dwight, and Earl and David Mixon...I wasn't there." It is amazing

———————————————————————————————

We will do anything to save our hides.

In this case, seeing the switch on the table in

front of Mother, saving my hide was not

just a figure of speech.

———————————————————————————————

how human beings will lie when caught, and even implicate their friends. We will do anything to save our hides. In this case, seeing the switch on the table in front of Mother, saving my hide was not just a figure of speech.

"I never swim in the drinking water." I lied again to Mother and repeated my innocence again and again. She probably believed the truth from Shakespeare: "Methinks thou dost protest too much."

Mother let me dig the hole a little deeper, then said, "Mrs. Hoffman saw you."

I should have known. Mrs. Hoffman saw everything and immediately told Mother. Everything.

Mother picked up the switch and slowly crept around the left side of the dining room table. Her steely blue eyes were unblinking. I knew the inevitable would happen. I remember the white cloth on the table, a pile of books and magazines on one corner and the ever-present pile of ironing on the other corner. Although it was inevitable I would get a switching, I responded as any kid would respond. I slowly edged around the right side of the table, keeping it between me and Mother.

"Don't run from me, you'll make it worse," she warned. But I continued to retreat around the table. "Don't run," she continued. Finally I froze in fear and she switched my legs till I cried.

"I'll never do it again," I cried, pleading with her to stop. It was humiliating to cry, but I could not hold back the tears. Afterward, I had to sit in the wicker rocking chair and think about what I had done. This was always Mother's way of teaching and correcting her son.

Sitting in the rocking chair, I always decided never to do it again, whatever it was I had done. Usually, however, I went back and did it again anyway. When I became a Christian, I understood what Paul meant when he said, "The good that I will to do, I do not do; but the evil I will not to do, that I practice" (Rom. 7:19).

Principles to Take Away

1. *The principle of self-image.* I did not learn who I was until I saw myself through the eyes of those who saw my youthful sin. I was happy when I thought no one saw me, but repentant when I was caught. I did not know who I was until I knew who I was not.
2. *The principle of the released self-image.* I had great freedom and enjoyment doing things that were prohibited, things I felt were not wrong, and things that did not hurt anyone. My rebellion told me I was in control of my destiny—that I had the freedom to be myself. Released from all restrictions, however, our self-image cannot mature as God would have it.
3. *The principle of guilt.* There are several kinds of guilt. I experienced *judicial* guilt by reviewing my actions against a standard or as explained by a judge (i.e., my mother). Judicial guilt kept me from the same act of rebellion (I never swam in the tank again), but guilt did not keep me from other acts (see the next chapter).

"Learning about authority and relationships—1944"

9

The Cornfield: When You're Hot, You're Not

I burned the corn in the field next to our house. It was not a huge amount of corn, but the event had a huge influence on my life.

The empty field next to our house was about the size of three city lots—less than half the size of a football field. Sergeant Sullivan, a county policeman, usually planted a crop in the field. He loved farming in his off hours. He also planted crops in other empty lots around the neighborhood. Gardening was his way of earning extra money. He plowed the fields with his mule, which he kept in a fenced lot by David Mixon's house behind the water tower. In the summer of 1944, Sergeant Sullivan planted corn next to our house. This was the cornfield that got burned.

I had just joined the Boy Scouts. Most of the Cat Patrol joined Troop 4 in East Savannah. Some of the boys from Garden Homes were also in Troop 4. A lot of rivalry existed between us boys from Wagner Heights and the boys from Garden Homes. It is amazing how I could hurl stones and curses at those Garden Homes scalawags; then a month later we would be laughing together as we learned to tie square knots to earn Boy Scout merit badges.

The merit badge system in the Boy Scouts introduced me to a whole new world. We were taught to pass tests such as reciting the Scout Pledge and memorizing the Scout commandments. We learned to live outdoors, and we had to pass tests such as cooking a meal outdoors.

I jumped into acquiring merit badges at a rigorous rate. First I became a Tenderfoot, which is the first rank one can reach as a Boy Scout. I bought the Scout shirt, and each time I earned a merit badge, Mother sewed it onto the appropriate spot. Each new rank also included a patch to be sewn onto my shirt. We never had enough money to buy the Scout hat, pants or the other parts of the uniform. But I was proud of my Boy Scout shirt.

A First-Class Scout Stunt

Next, I became a Second Class Scout. Then I went to work earning more merit badges to become a First Class Scout. At about this time I had to cook a meal outdoors over an open fire to acquire another merit badge. This involved cooking meat, vegetables and bread, and I had to provide a drink. That is when I burned Sergeant Sullivan's cornfield.

I had to find an appropriate place to cook outdoors. The Cat Patrol was sitting in my tree house discussing where we could cook a meal. We did not want to cook in my backyard because my mother would watch us and be too critical. We did not want to cook in the cemetery—signs were posted there forbidding open fires. The more we talked about it, the more difficulty we had in finding the right place.

Sitting there in the tree house, we also talked about what we would cook. "Let's cook corn and carrots," someone suggested. We talked about what we liked to eat. We really thought we could cook a meal as well as Mother could. "We've got carrots in my mom's garden, and they're ready for pulling," I said. I knew because I had planted them.

"Look at the corn," one of the Cat Patrol said. The tree house was built on the limbs of a pecan tree stretching out over the edge of the cornfield. Simultaneously, all eyes turned to see the field of green corn toasting in the hot Georgia sun. Suddenly we all knew where we would cook our meal.

"Yeah!"

"Let's do it!"

"Wow!"

So the Cat Patrol decided to "borrow" a little corn from the police sergeant, and we decided to cook it right in the middle of his cornfield, when the time came.

The fall of 1944 ushered in beautiful colors. The trees were washed with yellows, various shades of brown, and the green Southern pine needles became golden as they dropped to the earth. The green corn next to my house grew to enormous heights. At least it seemed tall to me. I had not yet heard the song about Kansas corn growing as high as an elephant's eye. The tall stalks also became as dry as tinder.

I rolled the blanket into a log roll, and tied it around the edge of the backpack. I looked like a French Foreign Legionnaire going across the desert.

The rows of corn were planted perpendicular to Wagner Street, meaning they were parallel with our house. Mother could not look out of her dining room window down a row of corn and see what was happening in the cornfield. The corn was so tall it blocked her vision. We knew we could play in the cornfield and be hidden from the omnipresent eyes of Erin Towns.

The Cornfield Feast

On a given day, I gathered the needed utensils: pots, frying pans, matches, wood and, of course, food. I wrapped the food carefully in wax paper, then packed everything into my backpack. We could not afford a brand-new Boy Scout backpack, so we went to the Army-Navy store and bought a used army backpack. After I had it all packed, I took the old coarse wool army blanket we had around the house. I rolled the blanket into a log roll, and tied it around the edge of the backpack. I looked like a French Foreign Legionnaire going across the desert.

I headed down Wagner Street toward the cemetery to throw Mother off the trail. I did not want her to see me going into the corn-field where we planned to cook our meal. Then I sneaked back into the cornfield and was the first of the Cat Patrol to arrive.

I smashed down several tall stalks of corn, being careful to pick the ears for cooking. A cornfield is rutted with deep rows. So I took the frying pan and used it as a shovel to smooth out a level spot for my fire.

Pop...pop...pop. The dry cornstalks cracked like falling timber when I broke them off at the ground. I pushed down a clearing about the size of the old scratchy army blanket, and spread it over the fallen corn. The brittle leaves snapped under the blanket when I sat down on it.

I dug a deep hole into the earth with the frying pan and poured in some water to make mud. Then I patted the wet mud around the potatoes until they were giant mud balls with potatoes inside. I put them back into the hole, along with several ears of corn. I covered the potatoes and corn with a thin layer of dirt, and built a fire over the food. I could imagine the tasty roasted potatoes and corn. I kindled a roaring fire with the dry cornstalks, and threw some dry branches on top to make some red-hot glowing coals.

For the meat entrée, I shaped ground meat into hamburgers. The pan that had been my shovel now became my frying pan. Of course, I washed it first.

One by one the Cat Patrol assembled at our secret destination in the center of the cornfield. I fried the hamburgers over the open flame, then used the pan for a shovel again to dig up the corn and potatoes. They were barely warm—still raw.

The meat was ready, however, and so were our appetites, so we ate hamburgers without vegetables. We still had to cook and eat vegetables though to earn our Boy Scout merit badges. So we rolled the corn and potatoes back into a mud covering, and threw more cornstalks on the fire to make it roar. We dropped the mud balls containing food into the fire, and sat down to wait for them to cook.

Because I have always been in a hurry, I thought they should be done immediately.

For a little while we lay on our backs looking into the sky. The scratchy army blanket made our sweating backs itch. The high clouds did not block out the red summer sunlight.

Waiting for our food to cook was hard for us. When children don't have a meaningful activity, what do they do? Girls put their heads together and giggle. Boys put their heads together and wrestle. Because we were typical boys, we began pushing one another and jumping on one another. We wrestled, had fun and laughed.

Running from Fire

Whether someone kicked a lit cornstalk into the standing corn, or a breeze blew a burning leaf into the field, I do not know.

"Fire!" someone yelled.

I grabbed the blanket and tried to beat out the flame. Instead of smothering the fire, the gust of air from the blanket when I swung it at the fire blew the flaming corn husks and leaves in every direction.

"Help!" I yelled.

"Get some water!" someone said.

"No! My mom'll see us," I protested.

We scooped dirt onto the fire with the frying pan and tried to stamp out the spreading flames. Luckily the wind was blowing toward Wagner Street and not our house or the Snyders' house. Soon we saw that we were fighting a losing battle.

"Pick up everything and run!" someone yelled. So I tried to cram everything into the backpack: the mud-covered potatoes and corn, pots, blankets and trash. I tried to kick the dirt back into place so people would not know we had been there.

"Run!"

We scattered into the cemetery as the fire began to burn itself out on the Wagner Street side of the field. We watched from our cave in the bamboo canes. We were afraid a fire engine would come, but it did not. We watched for a long time, but no one came to inspect the damage. What had seemed like a burning inferno was a flash fire that burned itself out quickly.

In the protection of our bamboo cane fort, we began to feel safe.

The Fire Department had not come. The police were not chasing us. Our parents were not yelling for us to come home. "It only burned part of the field," someone observed. Actually, the wind blew the fire due east to the street, and having no more dry corn to feed it the fire died.

"We're lucky," one of the guys commented.

"Yeah..."

"Nobody knows we did it."

"Yeah..."

"Did ya get everything from the camp?" one of the guys asked.

I had been the last one to leave, and I was sure I had picked up everything. "The fire burned up everything else," I said. "No one will ever know it was us."

It can be good to be frightened, for fear motivates us to take actions we would not ordinarily take. Fear can also motivate a young boy to repent.

We were all convinced that we had made a clean getaway. We watched silently. The longer we watched, the more we talked. That was a good sign, for we were losing our fear. It can be good to be frightened, for fear motivates us to take actions we would not ordinarily take. We would never have sat silently for more than an hour if our fears had not driven us into the bamboo canes for safety.

Fear can also motivate a young boy to repent. "I'll never do that again," I vowed. All of us evaluated our foolish actions, and determined we had been irresponsible.

"We shoulda' watched the fire."

"Yeah..."

After a while we could see no more smoke coming from the smoldering ashes. The emergency had ended. We had done all we could do. No one had been hurt. The only damage was that some corn had been burned.

We headed off into the cemetery to play. I do not remember what we played because our play was not filled with emotionally charged excitement, as was the fire incident. I can remember everything about the fire. I remember trying to beat out the flames and actually spreading the fire. I remember the panic. I remember running toward the bamboo as fast as I could and looking back as I ran to see who saw me. I will never forget sitting in the bamboo, scared to death. Then I experienced peace when no one came to look at the blackened spot where the fire burned some corn.

Facing Fire at Home

It was almost dark when I pushed open the screen door on the front porch at home. The fire was completely out of my mind. It could have happened a thousand years ago, for a short period of time is an eternity to a small boy.

"Hi Mom!" I called cheerily. She was sitting on the other side of the dining room table, and she was not glad to see me. I saw the switch on the table and knew that she knew.

"Did you see the burned field?" she asked straightforwardly, sounding like a trial lawyer closing in for the kill. "What happened?" she asked.

As Mother interrogated me I tried the innocent route, pretending I did not know what had happened. I had a way of lifting my eyebrows when I tried to hide something with a question.

"You burned up the corn," Mother accused me in no uncertain terms. I wanted to tell her the guys did it wrestling in the corn, but I was not ready to admit my guilt. I wanted to tell her it was a mistake and that I was sorry, but I could not bring myself to admit it. I saw the switch.

No one has to teach a small boy to lie. It comes naturally from the heart. When the Bible says, "All men are liars" (Ps. 116:11), it includes little boys; and they seem to lie the quickest.

"I didn't do it," I told Mother, trying not to panic. The fear I had experienced in the bamboo hideout returned, and I tried to hide it too. In the hideout, I had been afraid of the fire department, the police, Mr. Mixon who was in charge of the cemetery and Sergeant Sullivan who lost the corn. In the bamboo, I had fear in my bones. Now I had specific fear. I was afraid of my mother and what she might do to me. I looked at the switch and I looked at her.

"Why blame me?" I asked in my boyish naiveté. I still thought I could lie my way out of the matter by denying my responsibility.

"Mrs. Hoffman saw you and the others run," Mother said.

It's always Mrs. Hoffman, I thought to myself. She never misses a thing. Mrs. Hoffman is like God—she sees all things and knows everything. I found myself getting angry with Mrs. Hoffman for reporting me. I began walking around the left side of the dining room table as Mother went to the right.

"Don't run," she warned. "It'll only make it worse."

"I'll never do it again," I said pleadingly, trying that route. But Mother kept coming for me.

"Don't run," she continued to say.

"I'm sorry...I'm sorry...I'm sorry..."

She kept coming, though, and I eventually got my switching. According to the postmortem of the Cat Patrol, we all got a beating. I do not remember whether our families paid for the corn. Shortly the subject was dropped and never discussed again. Neither was swimming in the water tank.

Who Am I?

The relationship of a little boy with his friends is different from his relationship with his family. My mother taught me character, and my friends taught me relationships and how to get along with people. Both sets of teachings help children answer the question, Who am I? That is a question most of us have difficulty answering.

I was born clay—wet, moldable clay. Mother used every bit of her energy trying to mold pliable clay into character. I am also clay my friends molded into a member of the Cat Patrol. Sometimes my friends were my enemies, but in time my enemies became my friends.

Who am I? Among other things, I am a person who must balance the tension created by the expectations my friends put upon me, the expectations my parents put upon me and the standards I expect of myself.

Principles to Take Away

1. *The natural tendency-to-lie principle.* I found it was easy to lie when I got caught, so I know some people will lie to me when they get caught. I have learned the hard way to tell the truth, so I know not everyone lies when being caught.

Psalm 116:11 also says the statement "all men are liars" was made "in...haste."

2. *The principle of immature expediency.* I thought it was all right to sacrifice part of Sergeant Sullivan's cornfield so I could pass a Boy Scout merit badge. Immature people often think it is all right to do the wrong thing for the right purpose.

3. *The principle that correction may not transfer.* Just because I was punished for swimming in the water tank does not mean I learned not to camp in someone else's cornfield.

"I was a scalawag, especially at Halloween—1942"

10

Halloween: Doing What I Knew Was Wrong

As I have said, I was a member in good standing of the Cat Patrol, a group of about eight boys who lived in Wagner Heights, all within five blocks of my home. This informal group of boys was more of a social club than a "gang," as the term is used in the '90s. In the '40s, however, the Cat Patrol was the only gang of boys in my neighborhood. We never called ourselves "cats," and the term "cool cats" was not yet invented.

We were all proud to be identified as the Cat Patrol. In Jimmy Breland's favorite term, the Cat Patrol was a bunch of "scalawags"; but we considered the name a badge of honor.

We made our Cat Patrol emblems—a likeness of a cat's head with sharp-pointed ears—from the discarded wooden slats we found in the garbage of a man who lived on Helmkim Street. He had converted his two-car garage into a small factory, which was just a large workshop, where he crafted brown wooden venetian blinds with cream-colored cotton bands. We could always find broken venetian blind slats for swords, guns or the "cat" emblem. Using our pocket knives, we carved the thin slats into cat heads that had sharp cat ears. Using the sharp point of the blade we scratched whiskers.

Whenever we sandbagged a porch or soaped a window, we left behind the signature of the Cat Patrol. We thought we were sly and mysterious. We thought no one knew the identity of the members of the Cat Patrol. Unfortunately, everyone in the neighborhood knew who the gang members were. The effect of adding our "anonymous" signature to our practical jokes was largely lost.

Halloween was a particularly good time to get away with the normal activities of scalawags. Most of the people in the neighborhood expected their porches to be sandbagged and windows soaped on "All Saints' Eve." They usually protected themselves by taking valuable furniture inside.

A Disappointing Halloween Trick

Halloween night of 1942 was chilly, so I slipped on my black woolen jacket and pulled a dark woolen cap down over my ears. The Cat Patrol had chosen Mr. Saunders, the neighborhood grouch who lived on the corner of Mastick and Richardson streets, as our victim. We met at Harry Connelly's house and checked our weapons. We each had two paper sacks filled with sand, and a couple of rocks to rattle around on the porch after the sandbag hit its target. Of course it was night.

We crept through the darkness, staking out the house. Earl Fritz watched from Richardson Street. Dwight Arnold guarded the Mastick Street view from behind a long hedge between the house and the street. The streetlight was a challenge to our covert actions, so we sneaked behind three houses to make sure Mr. Saunders could not see us coming. We were sure he was squatting under one of the living room windows watching for us. I expected he might have a shotgun in his lap, so I was extra careful.

Harry Connelly, our leader, sneaked close to the front porch. When Earl Fritz, who was stationed on Richardson Street, gave the thumbs-up sign, we heaved a paper sack filled with sand and a few

---

"YEEEOOOPEEEUP!"

Eight juvenile voices yelled out through the night

our most bloodcurdling rebel yell, just as we

Southerners yelled at the battle of Bull Run.

---

rocks onto Mr. Saunders' wooden front porch.

"Thuuump!" The hollow sound was loud enough to awaken Mr. Saunders from sleep.

"YEEEOOOPEEEUP!" Eight juvenile voices yelled out through the night our most bloodcurdling rebel yell, just as we Southerners yelled at the battle of Bull Run.

We all ran pell-mell behind the Mullis house and waited for a furious Mr. Saunders to charge from his home and curse the darkness.

Nothing...no front-porch light flashing...no shotgun...no yells. Only silence.

If Mr. Saunders wanted to kill the enthusiasm of elementary school boys, he sure knew how to do it. He did nothing.

We shivered in the cool evening. It was about 7:30 P.M., not late by Halloween standards, so we decided to wait awhile and attack again. We were not, however, a unanimous decision-making body.

"Don't go—he'll be waiting," a fearful voice squeaked.

"He'll shoot," another scared kid said.

"Naw," someone else said. "He's asleep..."

The Second Sandbag Attack

Various opinions were shared and discussed. We decided I would lead the second paper-sack attack. I don't know who made the decision. Neither do I remember much about the sack, but it probably was like the first, containing mostly sand and a few rocks for noise.

I sneaked behind the Mullis house and down the common driveway they shared with Mr. Saunders. The Saunders house shielded the street light, so I crawled toward the front porch in the dark shadows. The only way I could have been detected was by my heavy breathing, the result not of running, but of sheer fear.

The front porch was high; it had seven steps leading up to the wooden floor. I crawled right up next to the front door, clutching my

---

Trying to turn and stop in one motion, I skidded on the gravel of the unpaved street and fell. Arms flailing wildly to the street to break the fall, I scraped flesh off my hands.

---

paper bag of sand and rocks. I was as scared as a GI sneaking up on a machine-gun nest carrying a hand grenade to blow away the enemy.

I looked across Mastick Street and got my signal from Harry—two flashes from his mother's flashlight. Then I looked down Richardson Street to see Earl Fritz and others behind a parked car. I got the thumbs-up sign.

I took off my tennis shoes, tied the strings together and hung them around my neck. I think I had seen a GI do that in a John Wayne movie. The soldier had to run through machine-gun fire to blow away the enemy. If the soldier could run faster barefooted, why not Elmer Towns? It never occurred to me that the soldier was running through sand, but my tennis shoes were designed for running on a city street.

I decided to throw my grenade—my paper sack of sand and rock—as high as I could so it would hit the porch harder and make a louder noise than it did the last time. A high-arching missile would also allow me to put my swift brave feet in gear more quickly for a running start to my escape. I figured to be across the street before the paper sack hit the porch.

I stepped out from the shadows and for a split second I faced the front door unarmed, except for the grenade. Would the enemy come charging out the door with weapons blazing?

Suddenly, I froze in fear. I could not throw my sack. I expected instantaneous death, but nothing happened. No Mr. Saunders...no porch light...no shot from the covering machine guns.

"Throw it, stupid!!!" I heard a squeaky preadolescent voice cut the night. The command shocked me to my senses and I lofted the sandbag high to get the effect I had planned. In the same motion I turned to run, my bare toes digging into the rocks of the dirt street. The tennis shoes flew out in centrifugal motion and bounced off into the middle of Mastick Street, illuminated clearly by the street.

My reaction was to run to the closest foxhole for safety and duck shotgun pellets. Then it flashed through my mind that Mr. Saunders might find my shoes and come after me. Trying to turn and stop in one motion, I skidded on the gravel of the unpaved street and fell. Arms flailing wildly to the street to break the fall, I scraped flesh off my hands.

I snatched the shoes and ran for darkness, crashing through the hedge on Richardson Street. Dropping my tennis shoes and having to go back for them made the getaway take longer than I had planned.

"I made it!" I reported breathlessly to Harry, like a soldier checking in with his sergeant. My chest was heaving from the life-threatening dash. My mind flashed from thought to thought, like a pinball that can't stop.

"I'm great! I ran the gauntlet and made it!"

"I'm safe! I wasn't shot!"

"I'm a hero!"

I had done what others had not dared to do. Then a puzzling thought coursed through my mind. Why weren't they yelling the Cat Patrol rebel yell? They were watching through the bushes. There was no, "YEEEOOOPEEEUP!" No one was slapping me on the back. No one was telling me what a brave act I had performed. They were ignoring me—looking through the bushes toward Mr. Saunders's house. I wondered what I would see when I looked through the hedge. Would I see a baffled Mr. Saunders holding a shotgun? Or bloodhounds? Had I broken a window? What was wrong?

I separated the hedge with two hands and viewed the wasted act of bravery, the missed opportunity for victory. My paper sack of sand had been thrown too high. It had landed on the porch roof. My careful thoughts about throwing it in a high arc had not taken into consideration the porch roof. I had missed the porch and hit the roof.

The Cat Patrol Punishment

We abandoned the sandbagging project for the night, but we did a thorough job of soaping screens and windows within reach. We returned to raid Mr. Saunders's front porch several times that evening. Finally, we littered the porch with the official club signature, the infamous cat's head. If nothing else, the dreaded symbol of the Cat Patrol would strike fear to his heart.

All was great fun for us until the next morning, when Mr. Saunders phoned Harry Connelly, the leader of the Cat Patrol. Mr. Saunders made it clear that we were to wash his windows, sweep his porch and hose down the screens. We were expected to finish the job that day, although it takes years to wash soap out of screens. I had to climb up onto the porch roof to retrieve the broken sandbag filled with rocks.

"If I tell your mothers, they'll beat you to death," Mr. Saunders threatened.

The Importance of Being Influential

Expressing the American democratic spirit, the Cat Patrol elected its leader periodically. Any member of the gang could be leader, but when the elections were held, Harry Connelly usually won. I always had leadership aspirations, and one day my day of ascension arrived. Political analysts might argue a mood for change prevailed among the gang members. Or perhaps Harry was just tired of being leader and wanted a break from the pressures of the office. The net result was that Elmer Towns was elected leader of the Cat Patrol. It all happened in the tree house in my backyard. Maybe the fact that they all ate lunch at my house had something to do with it.

As the newly elected leader, I decided we should have a rubber-gun fight. I began to divide the Cat Patrol into two teams. The thrill of power was great. I got to do what I always wanted to do. As president of the Cat Patrol, I did not have to worry about being picked last.

"Naw, I don't wanna," responded Harry Connelly to my directive.

"I'm gonna go to the movies." And with that, Harry and the other members of the Cat Patrol all went home to beg for nickels to get into the Savannah Theater. I was dumbfounded. I wanted to cry. I did what Harry wanted to do when he was president. Why couldn't he do what I wanted to do when I was president?

"It isn't fair," I pouted.

That day I learned a lesson about leadership. I learned that you can hold an office, but if no one follows you, you are not a leader. That day I learned an important difference between holding an office and being influential in the decision-making process. Years later, I turned down several opportunities to be president of Christian colleges because I wanted to be an influential educator, not just hold an office.

Today, I often tell my students, "I don't want to be famous. I just want to be influential." Sometimes my good friend Harold Willmington will encourage me by saying, "You're halfway there Elmer. You're not famous!"

Principles to Take Away

1. *The principle of hiding the obvious.* What we try to hide from others is usually known by them—and often ignored. Our desire to hide something from others reflects the emotional energy we attach to them, while their inattention reflects in inverse proportion their lack of concern.

2. *The insignificance of perceived epoch-making events.* The events we think are so great at the time are really insignificant when viewed through the eyes of history. What is important is friendship, acceptance by your peers and a sober view of your self-importance.

3. *The principle of leadership versus holding office.* When your friends follow you, you are the leader. They may elect you to office, but if they don't follow you, you are not their leader.

"The Cat Patrol"

11

The Cat Patrol: Being One of the Gang

The Cat Patrol was a great place to grow up because my buddies made me feel important. They made me feel like a human being.

The Other Side of the Tracks

I mentioned in chapter 9 that the Cat Patrol had a running battle with the boys of Garden Homes, the housing project three blocks from 107 Wagner Street where I lived. Garden Homes was built of large bricks on sandhills at the beginning of World War II. Poor families moved there from the small farms of central Georgia to work in the shipyards of Savannah. These families were usually struggling sharecroppers from farms having crops too meager to feed the family. The dads got government jobs and in many cases the mothers worked, so the kids ran free in the project and had little supervision.

I knew I was a member of the Cat Patrol from Wagner Heights and I definitely knew I did not belong to the Garden Homes gang. They were "poor white trash" in my mother's eyes. "You can't play in Garden Homes," she said, passing on her prejudices to me.

Only white children lived in Garden Homes in the segregated days of World War II. They attended Waters Avenue School where I attended. At school, we played with the boys of Garden Homes and they played with us. At least we could have individual play, but not group play. I especially liked two boys from Garden Homes—Joe Sigmon, whose father worked in the shipyard, and Charles McIntosh, whose father was overseas fighting in the war. The boys from Wagner Heights and Garden Homes got along well in school when it was one-on-one; but when we congregated as gangs, that was another matter.

"Meet at the mounds after school," we said, passing the word from one guy to another in the Cat Patrol. So after I came home from school, I drank a glass of milk—Mother wanted me to be healthy—and walked a block to Wheaton Street, crossed its concrete pavement, jumped a small ditch and walked out into the fields where "the mounds" were located. The mounds were nothing more than dump-truck loads of brickbats, blocks and rubble. They were a great place to play cowboys, and sometimes they became the Canadian Rockies when we played Royal Canadian Mounted Police. The mounds were dumped indiscriminately in the large field. From the top of one of the piles of rubble we had an excellent view of Garden Homes.

The large field between Wagner Heights and Garden Homes was cut in half by trolley-car tracks, and two deep ditches were cut on either side of the tracks. The ditches were as deep as a semitrailer truck, and it was hard to get in and out of them. The trolley-car tracks provided a geographical boundary between the Cat Patrol of Wagner Heights and the boys of Garden Homes. We seldom crossed the boundary to go play there, and I never remember their coming into our neighborhood.

Hurling Curses

When we met at the mounds, the eight boys from the Cat Patrol stood on our side of the trolley tracks and hurled curses at the Garden Homes "trash."

Because my mother thought the boys of Garden Homes did not have the moral standing of her son, she did not want me to play with them and told me I could not go there. What she did not know

---

The Cat Patrol had a corporate identity and a corporate conscience. As a gang, we took on a different personality than we had as individuals.

---

was that I could curse like a sailor, and that my language was as filthy as any boy from Garden Homes, word for word, term for term. I am certainly not proud of my language I used as a boy; I only describe its factual reality.

"You're one_____," I yelled at the guys at Garden Homes. "You're_____," they yelled back.

We never crossed the ditch as a gang. The Cat Patrol knew better. We did, however, go into Garden Homes individually. We went there one at a time to see a buddy. On several afternoons I went to play with Joe Sigmon, although, of course, I did not tell my mother.

The Cat Patrol had a corporate identity and a corporate conscience. As a gang, we took on a different personality than we had as individuals. When we were just sitting around talking, as we did up in my tree house, we did not use such filthy language. When we faced the Garden Homes gang, though, the Cat Patrol used the filthiest language. It seemed we cussed mainly to show off, not so much in day-to-day life.

The Cat Patrol did not go to the mounds to yell curses at the Garden Home "trash" every day, and we did not throw brickbats at them every day. Sometimes, however, the threats and yelling got louder than usual. Then someone threw a stone or a rock across the trolley tracks at the other gang. I define a stone as a small missile and a rock as a larger missile. A brickbat was part of a brick or a broken brick. They were heavier and small boys could not throw them as far. At least we could not get them across the trolley tracks and two ditches, so we reverted to throwing small stones.

Hurling Stones

As we were yelling our curses, we picked out the Garden Homes guy who was the loudest curser on the other side and threw stones at him. We almost never hit anyone, however, and we never suffered a direct hit. The distance from the mounds across the trolley track was half the length of a football field away. Even those of us who could throw a stone that far could not chuck it fast and true; it was more like a long lob. So our stones fell harmlessly among the Garden Homes boys.

When a stone was thrown at us, we generally waited until it was almost upon us, then we ducked or jumped out of the way. "Watch out—incoming artillery!" someone yelled. That was a phrase we had heard in the war movies we went to see at the Savannah Theater. We laughed as we dodged the incoming artillery. If anyone was hit, it was because he was not watching, or because a stone ricocheted crazily off the ground.

"Stupid bounce," I yelled one time, when a stone caught me right in the shin. In the Cat Patrol, however, you did not cry or let anyone know you were hurt. After all, John Wayne never cried when he got shot, so how could we do otherwise? When I got hit in the shin it stung right up to my eyes, and I almost cried in front of the guys. I did not look down, though, and more importantly, I did not rub it. We did not give the guys from Garden Homes the satisfaction of knowing they had hit us, or even hurt us. "Dirty guys always starting wars," I said and cursed them some more.

As a kid, it never occurred to me that the brickbats and stones came from the mounds on our side of the trolley tracks. The Garden Homes side was a field the government had leveled and plowed and planted with grass. It never occurred to me that they were throwing back the stones at us that we had first thrown at them. Only after I became an adult did I realize *we* were probably the ones who instigated the fights. As I reflect on my childhood, the guys from Garden Homes were just as nice as the guys from Wagner Heights.

Passing On Prejudices

About the prejudice I picked up from my Mother: Is it not true that much of our prejudice is passed on from parent to child?

After I became a minister, I met two other men who, we decided, were probably on the Garden Homes side of the trolley tracks, cursing me and throwing rocks at me. We laughed about it and today are ashamed of our cursing. Bill Brigmon graduated from the Liberty Bible Institute after retiring as an officer from the U.S. Navy. He had become a Christian and was serving the Lord. I would never have thought that a naval officer or a minister of the gospel could have come out of Garden Homes. The other man was a minister of Northside Baptist Church in Marietta, Georgia. He graduated from Baptist Bible College, and was a dear "saved brother" from Garden Homes on the other side of the tracks. He confessed to throwing stones at me. Now we serve the Lord together.

Neighborhood Acceptance of the Cat Patrol

"YEEEOOOPEEEUP!" was the rebel yell of the Cat Patrol. We saw one another a block away and launched out into what we thought was a bloodcurdling scream, "YEEEOOOPEEEUP!"

No one in Wagner Heights told us to be quiet or quit yelling. Everyone knew the boys had their own particular yell. Mother told me I could not yell in the house, but I could do it from the back porch.

Every lady in Wagner Heights knew all the boys in the Cat Patrol and kept an eye on us. They probably knew that we were just being boys, and that our rebel yell was harmless. I think the ladies of Wagner Heights liked us. After all—most of them fed us.

"Elmer...you want a cookie?" Mrs. Hoffman sometimes said as I cut through her yard on the way to Danny Waters's house.

The ladies of Wagner Heights felt a higher calling to keep the boys of the neighborhood straight. They seemed to be everywhere and to know everything we did. Maybe that is why we did not curse in Wagner Heights. We only cursed at the Garden Homes boys out on the field near the mounds. The ladies of Wagner Heights could not hear us there. In Wagner Heights, though, they seemed to see everything we did and hear everything we said. If we ever said something ugly, we heard a female voice yell from behind a kitchen window, "You boys behave or I'll phone your mother..."

That voice was usually enough to put the fear of God in any wayward soul. So we were careful what we did in Wagner Heights and how loud we cursed.

The ladies of Wagner Heights taught me that it is important to keep your eyes on children at play. Let them have their freedom and

---

Boyhood buddies are great to teach us about life and help us experiment. The way children get along with their friends reflects how they will get along in the adult world.

---

let them enjoy their friends, but do not let them hurt themselves, or harm other people—including the neighborhood water supply or a field of corn. When children make a mistake, handle it quickly and decisively, and make sure they learn an important lesson. Then forget about it and go on living.

The adults of Wagner Heights never branded me a "bad boy" or a troublemaker. I cut their grass, delivered their newspapers and waved when I rode my bicycle past their houses. I always said "Yes sir" or "Yes'm" in speaking with them. So thanks to the people of Wagner Heights who allowed the Cat Patrol and me to live among them and learn from their wisdom. My boyhood was good, and I learned lessons I will never forget.

The Importance of Boyhood Buddies

Boyhood buddies are great to teach us about life and help us experiment. The way children get along with their friends reflects how they will get along in the adult world. I learned that friendships are important and that we find identity in close relationships.

The Cat Patrol became my new family when I entered elementary school. I knew deep down that my mother loved me, but when she fussed at me for not getting home on time or for getting my clothes dirty, the Cat Patrol offered comradeship and acceptance.

None of my buddies in the Cat Patrol gave me a hard time, even though we slapped one another on the behind or punched each other on the shoulder. We were always "chewing" on each other or making meaningless threats such as, "I'll wipe out the toilet with you." We were buddies, though, and we really did not mean the harsh things we said to one another. When we fussed, I could yell back at them the way they were yelling at me. Mother's yelling was different. When she fussed at me I did not say anything except "Yes'm," and nodded my head dutifully.

I was not inwardly rebellious as were some children who said "Yes" with a smile but growled inwardly. Some kids got slapped around and hated their parents. You could see the hatred in these children in their squinted eyes, or on their downturned lips. You could just sense rebellion in their tone of voice.

"Yes'm" was always my verbal response when Mother got after me. Erin Towns was as clever as any trial lawyer. She not only won her case with her verbal demands, but she also won it by a quick word. She convinced me she was right—always right. So I always gave in, was obedient, believed her and said, "Yes'm."

When she made me a believer, though, I felt less than a boy. By always winning, my mother made me feel inadequate—a loser. Every time I said, "Yes'm," my self-esteem grew a little more tarnished.

Mother did tell me what a good son I was, and I believed her. She constantly reminded me, "You're a Towns, you're better than they are." I believed that, too. Whoever "they" were, I knew I was better because Mother told me so. When I was around my friends, however, I was just one of the other guys, and that felt great. We sat in my tree house because no one else had a tree house as big as mine; and we just talked or lied to one another.

"That's a P-39," somebody might say, pointing up to the sky at the sound of a single-engine plane flying overhead.

"Wow!" I said, because I had never seen a P-39. Then a twin-engine bomber approached Hunter Field over the marshes and flew low over Wagner Heights. The ground rumbled.

"That's a Liberator. That's a B-24." I lied to gain stature in the eyes of the Cat Patrol.

One of my buddies laughed and quipped, "Dummy! A B-24 is a British plane. We don't have any British planes here in the United States."

Then they all laughed.

"But I saw one yesterday...I really did." I swore to make my point. Then I tried to cover up. "At least I saw one that looked like a B-24."

We all laughed at one another's exaggerations, and sometimes we knew we were lying to one another. When we caught someone in a lie, we told him straight to his face, if it was a big lie. When it was a small lie, or marginal, or if we did not know whether it was a lie or not, then we let each other get away with it. Anyone could say what he wanted to; no one was excommunicated. Talking was no big deal; lying was no big deal; but to be a member of the Cat Patrol was a big deal. Boys learn who they are as they examine themselves through the eyes of their friends.

We laughed.

No one had to win to stay in the Cat Patrol, and no one was a loser. No one was kicked out. You could yell at someone and he yelled back, but we were buddies. You could argue with someone and he argued back, but in the Cat Patrol you had a chance to defend yourself, and that was important.

The few times I argued with my mother, I always lost. I could never defend myself. As a matter of fact, I could not argue with my mother much because she was always right. I could never present my side of the story. I could never change her mind because she had already made up her mind. She was right and I was wrong.

Principles to Take Away

1. *The principle of outer perception.* I learned that I was not what comes out of my mouth. I said many things because I was influenced by my friends; but I am what I think in my heart.

2. *The principle of seeing ourselves through our friends.* We gain self-perception when we see ourselves through the eyes of our friends. When I saw myself through the perception of my friends, it felt good and rewarding.

3. *The principle of necessary acceptance.* I learned that acceptance by your friends is necessary for happiness. I felt good about my friends.

4. *The principle of molding character by the "right" standard.* Character is habitually doing the right thing in the right way. As children grow through their rebellious phases of life, they need the stability of a parent who enforces the standard of doing the right thing in the right way.

Part IV

Uncles

Uncles, unlike our fathers, are male family role models who have little responsibility for us. Yet they still have a kind of semidetached authority over us, because "blood is thicker" than the rest of the stuff. They help nudge us into adulthood with their criticism or praise.

My uncles taught me to think differently about things than my father did. Although they all drank a little, except Uncle Herman, they told me not to become addicted to drink as my father had. They taught me that "men folks" can have fun. They did not order me around the way Mother and Daddy did, but gave me *reasons* for doing the right thing. They treated me like the young man they wanted me to become.

"My uncle taught me happiness in work"

12

Uncle Vernon: Finding Satisfaction in Milking Cows

When I was 12 years old, my mother let me do something I don't think any parents would let their children do today. I got on a Greyhound bus and rode it to Winsboro, South Carolina. I changed buses at Sumter, and went on to Columbia. There I changed buses again and went to Winsboro—all for the purpose of visiting my Aunt Ernestine and Uncle Vernon Timms.

Today, considering child kidnapping, child abuse and just plain vicious stupidity in the world, parents would not let their children do what Mother let me do. The South in 1944 was ruled by law. For the most part people were kind to children, and they obeyed the law. So Mother let me ride the bus 75 miles to the foothills of the Appalachians on the other side of Columbia, South Carolina.

Visiting a Dairy Farm

Uncle Vernon owned a small farm near the small town of Winsboro. He did not grow things for a living as did my uncles in Sardinia. He did not grow cotton, tobacco, peanuts or any other money crop. Uncle Vernon owned 22 cows, and was the sole proprietor of Bob's Dairy. I never asked why he called it Bob's Dairy. It was not his name, and he did not have a son named Bob. I guess it was just a name.

Each morning Uncle Vernon arose at about four o'clock, and his daughter, Ruth, and his wife, Ernestine, helped him milk 22 cows— at least the ones that were not dry. Aunt Ernestine only milked one cow. As soon as the three of them filled one bucket of milk, Aunt Ernestine carried that heavy thing up to the house where she pasteurized the milk in the kitchen.

The glass quart bottles had been sterilized the previous day. The kitchen table was cleared and this steel milk pasteurizer was set in place. After pasteurizing the milk, Aunt Ernestine filled each quart bottle and sealed it with a stopper on which was printed "Bob's Milk." The previous afternoon, buttermilk had been made by churning to extract the butter. Then the buttermilk was also bottled in glass quart bottles for delivery the next morning. Several quarts of buttermilk were ready every morning.

When I arrived at Uncle Vernon's farm, I knew I was not to get in the way. Milking cows was a twice-a-day chore, seven days a week. Cows give milk on Sunday, so that could not be a day of rest on a dairy farm.

"You sleep in tomorrow morning because you're not used to getting up," Uncle Vernon told me when we went to bed that first night. That was a slap in my face. Although I was only 12 years old, I had learned the lessons of mowing the lawn and working in the garden. I had learned that work could be fulfilling if you made up your mind to enjoy it. So I had made up my mind to get up and help with the milking.

"Wooh," I said the next morning when I came into the kitchen. "It's pitch black at four in the morning, even in the summertime." Uncle Vernon was up and going out the back door. He did not wait for me, or even pay any attention to me; he just got up and left. By the time I got dressed and headed for the milk barn, I was the last one there.

The milk barn was built of new concrete blocks and had a clean concrete floor. The only barns I had seen were old and dirty, and had dirt floors covered with manure and straw. They also stunk to high heaven. Later that day I saw Uncle Vernon's old barn. He kept a mule and a few pigs in the old barn; but the milk barn was new. The milk inspectors had threatened to shut them down because the old barn was so old and unsanitary. This new barn, however, had something I had never seen in a barn—electric lights, a bulb in each milk-

---

You do not pull, you squeeze, and your fingers must move from top to bottom as you pull. Then maybe, if you know what you are doing, the milk comes out.

---

ing stall and lights outside, on the front and back. My uncles in Sardinia had just installed electric lights in their houses, but they had not considered installing lights in their barns.

Krrr...krrr...krrr. I could hear the spew of steaming milk splashing on the bottom of a stainless steel bucket. I have never heard anything like it in my life. I walked around the other side of the cow to watch intently as Uncle Vernon's fat hands gripped the cow's teats and miraculously made milk spurt into the bucket. Because I was late, I had missed the preparation ritual. I had not seen Uncle Vernon bring the cow in place, wash her udder or place his stool in position to get ready for milking. He began the krrr...krrr...krrr as I walked into the barn.

I watched intently, wide eyed and filled with wonder at what I saw. I knew that cows were milked, and it looked to me to be a simple task. You just pull and the milk comes out. Later I was to find out that it is not as simple as it looks. You do not pull, you *squeeze*, and your fingers must move from top to bottom as you pull. Then maybe, if you know what you are doing, the milk comes out.

I found out that Uncle Vernon usually milked 14 cows, Ruth milked five, and Aunt Ernestine usually milked one. She helped get the milking started, then took the milk from her first cow into the kitchen, and left the two to finish.

Doing My Part

"Can I milk a cow?" I asked.

"Naw," Uncle Vernon responded. "This isn't play, this is work. This afternoon we might have a cow that we can teach you how on. But we've got t'get this milk out before eight o'clock this morning."

Krrr...krrr...krrr. Uncle Vernon kept on with the rhythmic process of pulling the life-giving liquid into the bucket.

I made myself useful by wrestling the heavy bucket up to the house, down a path that was about the length of a football field. That was helpful because Ruth usually did that job. Because I became the "milk carrier," she could help her father milk. So every time a bucket was filled, off to the farmhouse I trudged.

I wanted to stay around and watch Aunt Ernestine and the pasteurizing process, but she chided me, "Go get another bucket. We don't want the sun to find us late."

Aunt Ernestine was meticulously careful to make sure everything was spotlessly clean. From time to time, a state inspector came by, and if he shut them down they could not eat. They depended on the dairy for a living. "If the inspector wrote us up, people would stop buying our milk..." Uncle Vernon let the words trail off to nothing.

After milking, he used a hose to wash down the barn until it was cleaner than the house. I put the quart bottles of milk into the steel rack and took them out to the pickup truck. By the time I loaded all the milk into the truck, Aunt Ernestine had transformed the kitchen from a pasteurizing plant into a country kitchen. Eggs were waiting in a skillet on the stove, and grits was waiting in the pot. As we sat down, Uncle Vernon bowed his head and prayed, "Lord, make us grateful for this food we are about to eat. Pardon our sins. In Jesus' name, Amen."

Uncle Vernon drove a rusty black International pickup truck with rusting chrome bumpers and rusting chrome headlights. It looked like someone had beat it with a shovel. It sure did not look like a milk delivery wagon; I don't know what happened to the truck.

Back in Savannah, Georgia, Annette's Dairy had delivered milk to my house at 107 Wagner Street with a horse-drawn wagon. I forget the name of the horse, but it was as smart as the delivery man.

It walked from house to house down the dirt streets of Wagner Heights, stopping to wait for the delivery man as he ran from door to door depositing the bottles and picking up the empties.

Usually the horse started up again before the milkman got back to the wagon. It was not a wagon with the seat up high. Instead, the delivery man could step onto a platform only a few inches from the ground. Both sides of the platform in Annette's milk wagon were open, so he could go from one side of the street to the other. I remember once when a car hit and killed a milk-wagon horse, it made the front page of *The Savannah Evening Press*.

Back at Winsboro, my cousin Ruth and I sat in the front seat of Uncle Vernon's International pickup truck while we drove to town. Once in town, I rode in the back to deliver milk. Because my legs were young, Uncle Vernon let me run to the front door and deposit the milk in little wooden boxes he had built. I took out the empties, counted the money and ran back to the pickup. He kept the change in a cigar box on the dashboard, and the bills in his pocket.

While I rode in the back of the pickup truck, Uncle Vernon pointed to a house with his big, fat, muscular hand. At some of the houses, they requested a quart of buttermilk, a pint of cream or a pound of butter. Whatever the request, I ran back to the pickup truck, got what was needed and put the items into the wooden boxes by the door. Because I had delivered papers in Savannah, I knew something about the routine, so it was one of the enjoyable parts of living with Uncle Vernon. I liked delivering milk.

At one of the houses, I said to the lady who came to the front door, "Do you realize that you're going to drink milk that's only a few hours old?" I beamed with the pride of accomplishment as though I had completed the whole task, when actually I had done very little.

The lady looked at me with a condescending smile. Of course she bought Bob's Milk from Uncle Vernon Timms because it was fresh. Later I found out he boasted of the fact that he had never sold day-old milk.

Teachable Moments on the Front Porch

The first evening at Uncle Vernon's house was similar to a review for a final exam. We all sat on the front porch high on a hill overlooking the highway from Winsboro to Columbia. The sun was setting off to our left, which was west. Uncle Vernon did not talk much, but he listened for the unique sound of engines as cars or trucks came rumbling down the highway. Every once in a while he recognized the sputter of a pickup truck or the whine of an old Model-T and called the owner of the vehicle by name.

I was listening to a summer day drawing to a close. The crickets were tuning up as would an orchestra preparing for a concert. A loon off in the woods gave its low moan. It had been hot, but now the sun was setting and it was comfortable on the porch.

Uncle Vernon and Aunt Ernestine did not talk or tell stories as did my other aunts and uncles. They just sat and listened. I was listening for birds; Uncle Vernon was listening for cars and trucks.

"Uncle Buck got a weakness for the bottle," Uncle Vernon said to me. "He's kinda like your daddy. Your daddy likes to drink and it's going to ruin his life."

"Old Buck is going to get his nightly snort," Vernon said of a neighbor whose pickup was straining at the hill. The neighbor had a weakness for alcohol. I listened carefully to Uncle Vernon because he did not say much, but when he talked he said something worthwhile. I admired the dignity of his work. His house was his own. Although it was not new or fancy, it was his. As he sat on the porch, he enjoyed the accomplishments of the day, and I entered into his enjoyment vicariously. I thought of all the children in Winsboro who were becoming healthy because they drank Bob's Milk. I also thought of my role in making them healthy. I had wrestled buckets of milk to the kitchen and delivered bottles of milk to their front doors. Uncle Vernon felt good about the day, and so did I.

"Uncle Buck got a weakness for the bottle," Uncle Vernon said to me. "He's kinda like your daddy," he said, warming up to his commentary. "Your daddy likes to drink and it's going to ruin his life." He looked off into the distance, not at me. Uncle Vernon predicted that we might not have much money because eventually Daddy would drink it all up. Although I was 12 years young, I knew he spoke the truth because that was already happening in our family.

Mother and Father fought about money because we never had enough for groceries.

Uncle Vernon paused for a long time. This was an important time in the evening—another "teachable moment." My life was being changed.

"Young Elmer, if you learn to work hard you can amount to something in life," Uncle Vernon told me. "There's nothing so wonderful as to be able to sit down on your porch at the end of a hard day, and to know you've done your best." Uncle Vernon talked on at length about the virtues of work. I do not remember every word, but I remember the lessons.

Uncle Vernon's thoughts were still on the pickup that had driven around the bend. We could no longer hear the sound of the groaning engine and the hum of the tires. Uncle Vernon, however, was still thinking about the man he called Uncle Buck—although he was not really a relative—who drove into Winsboro to get drunk almost every night. We did not hear his pickup come back down the hill because we were asleep, but "Uncle Buck" came home drunk almost every night.

"Don't burn up your money smoking cigarettes, don't drink away your money on whiskey, work hard and you can amount to something in life." Uncle Vernon spoke directly now, looking at me. No gospel preacher was ever more effective with his sermon than was Uncle Vernon on the first night on his porch high above the highway between Winsboro and Columbia.

Principles to Take Away

1. *The principle of work-dignity.* Uncle Vernon taught me that I did not have to be rich to be respected. I learned the dignity of work—to gain respect by working hard.
2. *The principle of work-satisfaction.* Everyone wants to be happy, and I found my greatest satisfaction in being identified with a job and doing it well.
3. *The principle of work-contemplation.* Uncle Vernon taught me to sit down after the work is done and enjoy what I have accomplished.

"Learning to love vanilla—Uncle Herman in center"

13

Uncle Herman: Disliking Chocolate Ice Cream

My wife once asked me why I never ask for chocolate ice cream. I told her the story about Uncle Herman.

A Chocolate Ice Cream Feast

At one time I loved chocolate ice cream. Chocolate was also Uncle Herman's favorite flavor. We often made ice cream on our back steps in an old-fashioned hand churn in a wooden bucket.

One day, Uncle Herman phoned to ask my mother to make some chocolate milk custard for the ice cream churn. He said he was bringing the ice and the ice cream salt. He liked my mother's cooking. So Aunt Alice and Uncle Herman came to our house for supper. As soon as we finished eating, the chocolate custard was poured into the stainless steel canister and the dasher was put in place. The wooden barrel was packed with salt and ice.

Little boys churned first because it was easy to turn the handle before the ice cream hardened. The difficult part was left for the

That might have been one of the passages into manhood—the night I got ice cream in a soup bowl as large as Uncle Herman's.

grown men. So I began churning. Later, Uncle Herman finished.

"Don't churn so fast," Uncle Herman chided me. "Fast won't get it done any quicker."

Churning ice cream helped to digest the large supper we had just finished. Churning, though, does something else. Churning heightens your anticipation. It gets your taste buds working. The longer I churned, the better the chocolate ice cream tasted in my mind. A little chocolate custard bubbled out the top of the churn, so I wiped it off with a finger and licked off the chocolate.

"G-o-o-o-o-d!" I exaggerated the word to convince Uncle Herman how delicious the chocolate ice cream really was.

Uncle Herman took hold of the handle and continued to churn. Soon, but not soon enough, the handle did not turn anymore. The chocolate ice cream was hard. Mother unpacked the ice that was half melted, and removed the stainless steel canister full of chocolate ice cream. She pulled out the dasher—the paddle that swirled the liquid around until it hardened—placed it on a dinner plate, and gave it to me. Chocolate ice cream dripped all over the plate.

"I wanted that!" Uncle Herman kidded me. Everyone in the family knew the kids got the dasher. Using my spoon, I scraped the dasher clean of anything colored chocolate.

Uncle Herman got what he really wanted—a big soup bowl full

of chocolate. When I finished the dasher I spoke up.

"I'm ready for my bowl."

"Get him a soup bowl," Uncle Herman said.

That might have been one of the passages into manhood—the night I got ice cream in a soup bowl as large as Uncle Herman's. I had already had the dasher plate, but then I finished off a large soup bowl, not a smaller dessert bowl.

"That tasted like more," Uncle Herman said, winking at me. I grinned.

But we had eaten all the ice cream.

Too Much of a Good Thing

"We've got extra ice," Uncle Herman said. "Erin can whip up some more chocolate custard in two shakes of a lamb's tail." We all jumped into action, wanting more of that chocolate ice cream. That is, all except me. I was full of chocolate, but I did not want to say anything. Everyone else wanted more chocolate, so I said what they said.

I tell people, "Vanilla ice cream is God's favorite. God likes His ice cream simple, just like it comes from the cow."

"Chocolate...chocolate...I love chocolate..."

It took about 10 minutes to load the freezer, pack it with ice and start the freezing process. I was churning hard, hoping I could work off the extra chocolate. I also volunteered for extra churning.

After Uncle Herman started churning the freezer, I had to run around behind the house to make room for more chocolate. I was uncomfortably full.

Thirty minutes later, mother was pulling the dasher out of the churn. She passed it to me and the second helping was better than the first.

Uncle Herman filled his soup bowl full of chocolate and then scooped a full bowl for me. Then I got this terrible headache behind my right eye—the piercing pain that comes from eating too much, too cold, too quick.

I began to cry—I could not help myself. Uncle Herman laughed at me for eating too much, too cold, too fast. "Lie down," he said, his condescending voice directing me to the army cot in our dining room.

I lay down. Mother put a warm cloth on my forehead. My headache went away about the time my stomach knotted up. I doubled over on the cot and clutched my midsection. "Oooohhh," I let out a mournful wail.

Uncle Herman laughed, and whispered into my ear, "Want some more chocolate?"

"Oooohhh," I continued to moan.

"Stick your finger down your throat," Uncle Herman advised. "It'll make you throw up...you'll feel better."

I went to the back steps and tried to upchuck. "Ahaag..." Nothing came. I tried again. Still nothing. My stomachache only grew worse. In a little while, I broke out into a sweat all over my body. Mother removed the warm cloth from my forehead and brought a cool one. She ran for the thermometer, but I did not have a fever.

"He's got an old-fashioned stomachache," Uncle Herman concluded with a laugh.

I did not die, but I hurt a lot. I slept on the army cot that night in the dining room. My folks talked to Aunt Alice and Uncle Herman around the dining room table that evening. I remember fading in and out of wakefulness. Sleep was good because when I was asleep my stomach did not hurt.

As Uncle Herman left for the evening he yelled to me—lying there on the cot—"You want more chocolate?"

The question hurt as much as did my stomach.

A Plain Vanilla Life of Simple Joys

Many times after that, Uncle Herman kidded me about chocolate ice cream. Since that night, however, I have never again ordered it. It is not that I dislike chocolate, but I have learned to love vanilla ice cream more. As a matter of fact, vanilla has become my favorite.

A deep satisfaction is derived from the simple things in life—like vanilla ice cream. I sometimes tell people, "It's God's favorite." If they laugh, I say, "God likes His ice cream simple, just like it comes from the cow."

All the uncles on my daddy's side (the Towns family), except Uncle Herman, died as helpless drunks, most of them of cirrhosis of the liver. I once asked Uncle Herman why he quit drinking. He told me, "I didn't like getting sick and vomiting...I hated it when I fell on the front porch and couldn't get into the house...I hated sneaking a drink...and I hated being poor."

Uncle Herman told me, "When you get sick enough, you look for what you like."

I understood what he was saying. I got sick of chocolate ice cream and never ordered it again. I chose vanilla instead.

In a similar way, I got sick of my father's drunkenness. It was obnoxious. I wanted a pure life, and I wanted vanilla.

Daddy was miserable. The bottle never made him happy; it just helped him escape. I saw his misery and I opted for a plain vanilla life of simple joys.

Principles to Take Away

1. *The principle of saturated satisfaction.* I learned that when you get too much of a good thing, it loses its luster and appeal. The thing you crave is not as attractive when you have too much of it.

2. *The principle of destroyed desire.* I learned that it was not getting what I wanted that gave me the most happiness. I was happiest when I lived desiring something. Unfulfilled desire is a good condition, for it gives meaning to life and drives us to live.

3. *The principle of reverse satisfaction.* I learned that when you become nauseated from too much of a good thing, you turn against it.

"Uncle Sam McFaddin—1917"

14

Uncle Sam: Stories that Were Sometimes True

Technically, my Uncle Sam was not my uncle. He was actually my grandfather's stepbrother. I called him Uncle Sam because everyone else did. He was the greatest storyteller in the family. He loved to gather all the kids around his feet as he sat in the rocker on the front porch, just to spin a yarn.

A Captivating Storyteller

Samuel McFaddin was the father of my Aunt Alford McFaddin, who married Uncle Gene, my mother's brother. Uncle Sam dressed the part of a storyteller. He always wore a Palm Beach double-breasted suit the color of vanilla ice cream, a white shirt, a black string tie and black shoes. Uncle Sam dressed like a skinny Colonel Sanders. He had the same infectious smile behind the white goatee on his chin, and wore a long white mustache.

"He's the laziest man I've ever known," his daughter, Aunt Alford, said about him. None of us kids ever thought about it though. We loved to hear his stories, especially the way he described people.

When Uncle Sam told a story, he always sat on the edge of the rocking chair, leaning forward on his walking stick. "Now look me in the eye," he commanded, in a high tenor voice that scratched. When we did not look him in the eye, he said, "How can I tell you a story when you're not listening with your eyes?" Sometimes we watched a car drive down the Kingstreet road. Anything that distracted us irritated Uncle Sam.

The Story of the Yankee Soldiers

One day Uncle Sam sat on the front porch of my grandpa's house. No other grown-ups were around, so he called us kids together for a story. He especially liked to tell stories when no other adults were around to hold him accountable.

"Younguns," he said, "look down the lane." We stood on our "tippy toes" to see who was coming down the lane, but no one was coming.

"Younguns," Uncle Sam continued, "I remember the day I saw two Yankees comin' down dat lane."

Uncle Sam had a glint in his eye as he set the scene for us. "Sit real close and listen with your eyes, and I'll tell you about how we saved the place from the Yankees." Everyone called Grandpa's house "the place" or "up home." I had heard something about this story. An older cousin had mentioned the Yankees who got shot on "the place," but he just laughed and did not tell me the story. Now I knew I was about hear it.

"I was just a young teenager when I heard the Yankees had burned a strip a mile wide from Atlanta to Savannah during the Civil War." Uncle Sam cautioned us to watch him carefully. He warned us that if we did not listen with our eyes and listen with our minds, the story would stop.

"Quiet, y'all," I piped up.

Uncle Sam explained that he had been left to work the fields for the women when the men went off to the Civil War.

"After the Yankees took Savannah," Uncle Sam lowered his voice so we had to listen carefully, "they began marching up through the low country of South Carolina looking for plantations

---

"These two Yankee soldiers came riding down the Kingstreet road riding fat horses," Uncle Sam continued. "They were looking for houses to rob and then burn."

---

to burn." The low country was filled with plantations such as my grandpa's before they were burned to the ground.

"So we hid the silverware and anything else that was valuable down in the swamp by the branch." The branch was a creek that wound its way through the low wet woods we called a swamp.

Uncle Sam paused at the right place, to rivet any eye that began to wander. My cousin Paul David O'Cain was not listening, so Uncle Sam leaned on his walking stick and asked, "Do you want me to tell you about shooting the two Yankees, or not?"

We rhythmically nodded our heads yes, my flattop bobbing up and down. My haircut was a flattop because it was during World War II, when that was the thing to do. We had been sweating in the sun playing army, and we were hot and probably dirty. Because we had been playing army, we were in the mood to hear about the day war came to Sardinia and how Uncle Sam shot the Yankees.

"These two Yankee soldiers came riding down the Kingstreet road riding fat horses," Uncle Sam continued. "They were looking for houses to rob and then burn. The officer was on a gray mare, and he looked down our lane. He probably thought the menfolks were still off at the war defending our nation. The enlisted man with him had cloth bags hanging from the saddle. They were filled with money, clocks and anything else they could steal from the good folks of South Carolina."

Uncle Sam always knew how to drag out a story, as well as how to set it up. He told us how they had seen the two Yankee soldiers stop on the Kingstreet road as though they were trying to decide whether they should come down our lane or head toward Sumter.

Uncle Sam was the older of two teenage boys who watched the two Yankee soldiers. He was 15, and his cousin Jason was 12.

Wow! I thought. *I'm 11...just one year younger.* Here I was 80 years later, dreaming about the Civil War. I wondered if I could draw a bead on a man and pull the trigger. Could I kill a person? I asked myself as I listened to Uncle Sam's story.

Uncle Sam and Jason watched the two Yankees carefully. They hoped the soldiers would keep on going to Sumter. When they turned in the lane toward Grandpa's house, Uncle Sam said to Jason, "Let's get ready..."

The lane to Grandpa's house ran 100 yards from the Kingstreet road straight up to his house. Under the tree in the front yard was a place for wagons. Then the lane angled off to the right so horses and people could ride between the main house and the tobacco pack house. The main house had a picket fence all the way around it. The tobacco pack house had a chicken-wire fence around it, and the lane passed between the picket fence and the chicken-wire fence.

Uncle Sam described the two Yankees as they rode into the front yard. "The officer stopped first, looking for any sign of life. He didn't see anything move. Even the dogs and chickens were quiet, knowing it was dangerous to move.

"The officer had a yellow mustache that was stained brown with tobacco juice. He spit on the dry ground, raising a puff of powdery dust. Then he wiped his mustache with the back of his gloved hand, and wiped the juice off his glove onto the horse's rump."

Uncle Sam stopped his narrative to give us some background. He told us he had the Yankee officer in his rifle sights, but he was afraid to shoot because if he only wounded him, they would go for help and return to kill them, rape the womenfolk and burn down the place.

"I knew I wouldn't miss," Uncle Sam said, "but I didn't know if we could knock them off their horses.

"Those two Yankees moved their horses in slowly between Grandpa's house and the pack house, between the two fences. They carried their rifles across their saddle horns, ready for trouble. They didn't see me in your grandpa's bedroom, sitting there with a muz zle-loading long musket.

"I knew when I pulled the trigger it would knock me down, but I'd blow a hole in that Yankee big enough to put your fist through. And Jason, he'd hidden over in the pack house. When they cut between the two fences, we would have them in our cross fire."

Uncle Sam described how he felt. "I was a little scared. I had

---

Uncle Sam explained, "Of course it wasn't wrong to kill a Yankee, because the Yankee was going to burn your house to the ground."

---

never shot anyone before, and I didn't know what it would feel like to kill a man." Then Uncle Sam explained, "Of course it wasn't wrong to kill a Yankee, because the Yankee was going to burn your house to the ground."

Uncle Sam described sitting in my grandpa's bedroom, looking out the window at these two Yankees not more than 20 feet away. "They were so close I could see that officer's blue eyes behind that yellow mustache." He described the sweat dripping from the officer's forehead.

"I only had one shot in my rifle," he continued, adding that he knew that if he shot and missed, the Yankee would kill him. Then Uncle Sam reminded us that he could knock a squirrel out of the top of a tree when all he could see was its head popping up from behind the fork of the tree.

Uncle Sam explained his dilemma. "I was worried that Jason would miss...or get scared and not pull the trigger.

"When the soldiers got to the back of the house, they were in a perfect cross fire between Grandpa's bedroom and the tobacco pack house. Kaboom! rang out my muzzle loader, and fire belched from the end of the barrel. The officer dropped like a bale of cotton off a wagon. He never felt a thing. Then, just that quickly, Blam! and Jason's squirrel gun barked like a hit dog. The enlisted man spurred his horse, but it only ran a few yards. Then he slid off his fat horse, twitched in the dirt, and died."

I remember being stunned into silence, listening with my eyes fixed on Uncle Sam's kind face. One of the other kids asked, "Were they really dead?"

"Dead as cockroaches stepped on by a boot," Uncle Sam said.

"Whatja do?" another one of my cousins asked.

The Sweet Grapes from the Scuppernong Grapevine

Uncle Sam stroked his chin whiskers and took one hand off his walking cane. He pointed over beyond the picket fence, across the lane and the chicken-wire fence, to a grapevine. "See that grape arbor?"

All of us children sat upright up on the front porch to look at the grape arbor. "There's a reason why that grape arbor grows black grapes and all the other vines grow white scuppernongs," Uncle Sam said.

Seven grape arbors were located on my grandpa's farm. These were not just grapevines growing perpendicular to the ground as those found in California. In the South, these grapevines grew on arbors, stretched out flat on a network of sticks and pipes built about five feet off the ground. We walked under the grape arbors and reached up to pick the grapes. The grape arbors were great places for shade. My grandfather had six white scuppernong grape arbors, from which he made white scuppernong grape wine each September. The other arbor, halfway between Grandpa's bedroom and the tobacco warehouse, grew black scuppernong grapes.

"We buried those Yankees right there under the black scuppernong grapevine," Uncle Sam told us kids. "And that vine has always produced the sweetest grapes of any of our grapevines." I knew that was true because I went there first for grapes.

"Yankee fertilizer makes those grapes better than the rest," Uncle Sam told us.

Learning the Truth

The story of the two dead Yankees buried under the black scuppernong grapevine located halfway between Grandpa's bedroom and the tobacco pack house was a family secret. We did not talk about it much because the Bible said, "Thou shalt not kill." As a matter of fact, I never told the story as long as Uncle Sam was alive. I did not want to get him into trouble, and I did not want Yankees to think I was prejudiced.

When I was about 55 years old, I was sitting in my mother's kitchen talking with Aunt Leila about Uncle Sam. In our conversation, someone mentioned that he was born in 1866.

"Wait!!!" I said with anguish of soul. "You mean to tell me that Uncle Sam was born the year after the Civil War was over?"

Aunt Leila and Mother nodded their heads yes. They wanted to know why was I so upset. Then I told them the story about the two Yankees buried under the black scuppernong vine halfway between the tobacco pack house and Grandpa's bedroom.

They laughed.

Sure enough, Uncle Sam was born the year after the Civil War ended. The house where the Yankees were supposedly shot, my grandpa's house, was not built until 1889—25 years after the Civil War ended.

Mother reminded me that Uncle Sam always told stories, and that some of them were true. Some of my relatives think the story *is* essentially true, but that it happened to a younger McFaddin a generation earlier, and that it happened at my great grandfather's house on the road that ran between Kingstreet and Sumter. My great grandfather was named Robert E. Lee McFaddin, and my grandfather was Robert Ely McFaddin.

Principles to Take Away

1. *The principle of vicarious stories.* Uncle Sam taught me that children put a lot of stock in stories, and that through them they relive the lives of the people they hear about.
2. *The principle of identificational storytelling.* Uncle Sam taught me that some storytellers get so wrapped up in a story that they project themselves into scenes in which they never actually lived. There is a thin line between artistic identification and deceiving your hearers.
3. *The principle of multilevel stories.* I learned that listeners hear the story at a different level of reality than does the teller. Although Uncle Sam was reliving the story he probably heard from real Civil War observers, I relived it at a modern level, and interpreted it to my own world.

"Where Uncle Sam greeted folks"

15

Uncle Sam:
The Laziest of Them All

My Uncle Sam went to bed early each evening. He did not sit on the porch in the evening with adults and swap stories. I guess he enjoyed the individual attention of the children when adults were working. As I said, he probably did not want the grown-ups correcting his stories. He went to bed early and arose late, and lived until he was 92.

"He's the laziest man I've ever known," his daughter, Alford, said out of earshot of Uncle Sam. She loved him and did not want to hurt him.

Gentlemanly Craftiness

Maybe Uncle Sam was crafty instead of lazy. When he was about 50 years old, he was so deathly sick that he could not work his farm. So he called his three children—Alford, Ray and Cecil—to explain to them that he was too sick to work. He proposed dividing up the inheritance among his children while he was still alive.

"Alford," he said to his daughter, "I will give you my house in Sardinia, the store and the grits mill." To Cecil he said, "You can

Southerners look on grits with religious fanaticism because it had "saved" them. Grits kept them alive during the Great Depression when nothing else was available except sweet potatoes and some chickens in the backyard.

have the farmland." And his other son, Ray, got the old homestead on the road to Kingstreet, South Carolina.

Everyone said Alford got the best part of the deal. Only one store was located in Sardinia, which Uncle Sam owned, and it was a moneymaker. In addition to selling groceries, the store housed the Post Office in one corner. The U.S. mail was delivered there, and before he gave the store to Alford, Uncle Sam was the postmaster for the whole area. Everybody came to his store to pick up the mail, and they usually bought something while they were there. The store didn't have a name; it was just "the store."

The Grits Mill: A Lifesaver

Across the dirt road from the store was a tin building called "the grits mill." People brought their corn to Uncle Sam's mill to be ground into grits, and Uncle Sam got part of the grits to sell in his store. Every Saturday morning around six o'clock, the single-piston steam engine in the mill fired up. I remember awakening on many Saturday mornings to the rhythmic music of the grits mill. Pow...pow...pow. It could be heard everywhere in Sardinia for hours on end.

All through Saturday morning and into the early afternoon, the whole town could hear the music of the grits mill grinding corn into the life-saving recipe that was simply called grits, or "southern ice cream." When the deep depression hit and people had nothing to eat, they could always grind their corn into grits and live off it.

I once had a Canadian student who criticized grits and Southerners who ate it. My Canadian student did not understand that Southerners look on grits with religious fanaticism because it had "saved" them. It is more than food to the true Southerner. Grits kept them alive during the Great Depression when nothing else was available except sweet potatoes and some chickens in the backyard. Many Southern sharecroppers ate only grits and fried fat meat for breakfast.

The sharecroppers began arriving at the tin-covered grits mill, as I said, at about 6:00 A.M., in their wagons drawn by a single mule. They usually brought a single bag of corn to be ground into grits. Most did not bring too much corn to be ground at one time because fresh grits taste better than do stale grits. As well, the older grits get the more likely bugs are to invade it.

Uncle Sam could grind grits into two different levels of coarseness. The first was coarse grind, which made what is actually called "grits." Southerners boiled it in water and added butter, gravy or sometimes meat juice.

The second grind produced a much finer meal some people called "hominy." My Mother called it "gruel." She stirred it slowly into a pot of boiling water so that it became creamy, almost like Cream of Wheat, only it was cream of corn. Mother served it in a bowl and added milk, and we called it "gruel soup." On a typical day, we ate grits for breakfast, but whenever I became sick Mother cooked gruel because it was creamier. She also maintained it had therapeutic value. Maybe it just made us feel better because we thought we were being healed.

Bargaining for a Secure Life

Along with the grits mill and the store, Uncle Sam gave the first large house on the only street of Sardinia to his daughter, Alford. The wooden house had four large bedrooms—each bedroom had a fireplace—a dark living room, a dining room and an extra-large kitchen. The house also had tall ceilings; it was always dusty, and the yellow paint was dirty throughout the house. Heavy blinds and shades were drawn to keep out the blistering Southern sun so the house could remain cool during the day.

When Uncle Sam became sick in the fiftieth year of his life, he not only talked to his children about their inheritance, but he also bargained with them. He offered his daughter the house, the store and the grits mill if she would sign a document to take care of him the rest of his life. He made the same arrangement with his son Ray, who received the old homestead and its good farmland.

Then Uncle Sam turned to his son Cecil and said, "I'll give you the farm. It stretches from the highway all the way to the Black River. It doesn't have a house, so you'll have to build one." Uncle Sam was one of the richest landowners in the area. He bargained with his son Cecil just as he had with Alford and Ray. "I'll give you the farmland," he said, "if you'll sign the paper to take care of me while I'm sick, for the rest of my life...until I die."

Uncle Sam worked out a deal so he would stay a week at Alford's house, then a week at Cecil's house and a week at Ray's. They were to provide his food, buy his clothes, wash his clothes and give him spending money.

So with that understanding, his children Alford, Ray and Cecil signed the paper. As you already know, he did not die right away. Uncle Sam lived for another 42 years—until he was 92—and did not do another lick of work the rest of his life. Yet his vanilla-colored double-breasted suit was always clean, and if you looked carefully you could tell that the collar of the white shirt he wore every day was never dirty

"I never saw him break a sweat again," is the way Uncle Cecil put it.

A Comfortable Daily Routine for "the Mayor"

Each morning Uncle Sam got up around eight o'clock—a couple of hours after the other menfolk had awakened and gone off to the fields to work. As a little kid, I usually got up with my Uncle Gene to go with him to the fields. When I did stay home with Aunt

Alford, I saw Uncle Sam get up around 8:00 A.M. Aunt Alford cooked breakfast for him, then he put on his vanilla double-breasted suit and tie (the string tie). He picked up his walking stick and strolled about 100 yards down the sandy road to the Post Office.

Uncle Sam always arrived there by the time the mail came in at 10:05 A.M. He waved at the mailman, cousin Dub McFaddin. Mailman Dub drove a large Buick sedan that had an air horn so loud that he would announce his arrival a mile before he reached the store in Sardinia. Dub dragged a bag of mail out of the trunk of the car and gave it to Wilbur, the man who had taken the job of post-master from Uncle Sam.

Then Dub took the bag of outgoing mail and threw it into the backseat. He always took the cushion out of the backseat so the mailbag would not get it dirty. He wanted to use the car on Sunday to go to church. Dub never got the bags mixed up. Incoming mail was placed in the trunk, outgoing mail in the backseat.

After the mail arrived, Uncle Sam took his place on a wooden bench right next to the front door. From his seat, he greeted everyone who came for the mail—and that was everyone, every day.

Sardinia had never elected a mayor because it was an unincorporated village. It occupied only one street, on which were located six houses, a grits mill, Uncle Sam's store and a Presbyterian church and parsonage. From the town of Sardinia, I could look five or six directions and maybe see another five or six farmhouses, but that was it. Sardinia was small-town America and had an unofficial mayor—Uncle Sam. Daily "the mayor" sat in his official seat on the bench to the right of the front door of the store.

The old wooden store was not painted as far back as I remember it as a boy. I went past there 50 years later and it still had not been painted. The wood absorbed every smell of ham, barbecue, cheese or anything else that drifted by. It always had a musty smell, and the floor was permanently covered with sand tracked in from the sandy yards in the front and back of the store. The front yard was also covered with bottle caps from all kinds of pop, some rusty, some as shiny as the day they were popped off a Double Cola or Grapette.

When people bought a cold drink at the store, they sailed the cap out the front or backdoor. Neither one had a screen door. When it rained, a car never got stuck at the store because the bottle caps gave the tires traction in the wet sand, the way gravel does today.

The Town's Cheerful Greeter

Uncle Sam performed the ritual of greeting people coming and going the way a preacher greets everyone who leaves church after a sermon, calling people by name or asking about their children or neighbors.

"How's Lem's chicken pox?" he sang out when Aunt Hazel came into the store.

"I see you're building a new tobacco barn," he said to Bruce Fleming because he wanted to pass gossip on to everyone who came or left.

My mother and Aunt Alford called Uncle Sam lazy, but everyone liked him. Just like the two sides of Dr. Jekyll and Mr. Hyde, at times I wanted to be like Uncle Sam.

He's smart, I thought. *He just sits and everyone waits on him.* A part of me admired an uncle who had nothing to do but sit around in clean clothes and tell stories to children. (Some of them were true.) Another side of my thinking, however, was, *I don't want people to look down on me for being lazy.* Even as a 12-year-old, I wrestled with self-perception and life goals.

Principles to Take Away

1. *The principle of indigenous security.* I respect Uncle Sam for being wise enough to plan for the future. He conceived of a future that fit his indigenous approach to life, and he lived happily in his own world. Although I could not be happy doing what he did, just knowing Uncle Sam brought pleasure.

2. *The self-reflective principle.* Uncle Sam dressed the way he wanted other people to think about him, and he did those things he knew they expected of him. He enjoyed seeing himself reflected in their expectations.

My aunt and uncle taught me tolerance

16

Uncle Johnny: The Henpecked Hero

My Uncle Johnny taught me something on a Sunday afternoon in Burroughs, Georgia, that I never forgot. It was about everybody's need to be somebody.

"Let's walk down to the warehouse," he said with a twinkle in his eye. A potato warehouse was located on a railroad siding about a 10-minute walk from his house down the main tracks of the Atlantic Coastline Railroad. To understand Uncle Johnny, you have to know about his passion for power over both railway cars and little boys.

Uncle Johnny was a skinny short man in his 50s, and he had a bald head and a thick graying mustache. He looked Greek or Italian, but he wasn't. He could have been Corsican because the broad-brimmed straw hat he wore to cover his bald head made him look like the Mafia stereotype.

Uncle Johnny had a reason for being a boy among the men in the family, and a man among the boys. He had a reason for choosing the warehouse to tell me and my cousins those fantastic stories about World War I. He sat on a pile of potatoes and told how he shot seven Germans. I do not know how many times I heard that story as a boy. Uncle Johnny loved to tell stories to kids, but around the grown-ups he did not say much. The reason? Aunt Pauline.

My Father's "BIG Sister"

Johnny was married to my Aunt Pauline Newsome, my father's big sister. Southerners use the descriptive phrase "big sister" to mean older sister. When I say she was my father's big sister, however, I mean BIG. She not only was older than both my father and her husband, Uncle Johnny, but also her shoulders and hips were wider, and her voice dominated a family reunion table conversation.

Aunt Pauline was not fat, the way a pro-football linebacker is not fat. A linebacker is muscular, big boned, and standing above you, he intimidates you. Just like Aunt Pauline. When I think of Aunt Pauline, I shake my head in unbelief because I know people won't believe what I say about her. I shake my head and laugh. Aunt Pauline gave new meaning to the word "odd."

Uncle Johnny worked for the Atlantic Coastline Railroad, so Aunt Pauline was always traveling somewhere on a free pass. Only two trains stopped each day in Burroughs, a small community that had only one store and a dirt road that crossed the tracks. One train left early each morning for Savannah and the other left Savannah late at night on the way back to Burroughs. So Aunt Pauline often went to Savannah to stay all day with her relatives. She phoned my daddy early in the morning from the Union Station.

"I'm at the station. Come get me," she demanded.

"No," I heard Daddy say into the black upright phone.

He then put one hand over the wide mouthpiece and told Mother, "It's Pauline..." They both rolled their eyes in exasperation.

My father spoke again into the upright phone and told his big sister, "I told you we can't drive you all over Savannah just because you decide to spend the day in town." He explained she had to phone ahead because he had plans. "Catch the cab," Daddy told her, but she usually did not do it because it cost 35 cents.

One morning, however, she did catch the cab, and the stories of that Saturday morning are legendary. On Saturday, we usually slept in until 7:00 or 8:00 A.M., and to compound the problem we did not

---

The whole house was rocking with a rollicking rendition of the "Minute Waltz" played as if by a drunken piano player in a dance hall. Even in church, Aunt Pauline could pound the ivories and make "Amazing Grace" bounce to a boogie beat.

---

lock our doors. No one did in our neighborhood in Savannah when I was a kid. We just walked in on friends and yelled, "Ya'll home?" Other than for acquaintances, though, we knocked.

Aunt Pauline did neither.

We were all sound asleep on a Saturday morning, when we awoke to a loud banging on the piano. The whole house was rocking with a rollicking rendition of the "Minute Waltz" played as if by a drunken piano player in a dance hall. Even in church, Aunt Pauline could pound the ivories and make "Amazing Grace" bounce to a boogie beat.

"What the #%&*!!" Daddy cursed, charging into the living room to see Aunt Pauline grinning from under a wide, black-brimmed straw hat covered with artificial plastic fruit. Seeing her younger brother, she began to sing. He continued cursing, which was amazing. My father did not curse around women and children, but that morning I broadened my vocabulary to include a few spicy terms.

Talk about funny. Aunt Pauline screeched off-key. She hammered the keys as though she had a grudge against them, often missing a few. I said she was my father's big sister—her well-endowed chest glands alternated with her flaying hands at landing on the piano keys.

I could tell stories about Aunt Pauline...

Aunt Pauline Meets My Wife

After Ruth and I were married, Aunt Pauline came to visit us in St. Louis, Missouri—on a free pass, naturally. She phoned me from the train station, naturally. Ruth had never met Aunt Pauline, but she remembered receiving a wedding present from her. It was a beautiful piece of gold tapestry about three-feet square, and a corner was cut out.

"What's this for?" Ruth asked, a little sarcastically—which was out of character because Ruth is a gentle woman who speaks well of all people. Except Pauline.

"It's lovely," Ruth told Aunt Pauline on the phone, "What did you have in mind?"

"You can cover a pillow with it," Pauline answered.

So when Aunt Pauline came to visit us in St. Louis, Ruth was expecting the worst—and she was not surprised. Almost immediately, Pauline washed her bra and panties in the sink and hung them over our front-porch rail. Although Ruth did not realize it at first, they hung there fluttering in the breeze all morning. What a topic for our neighbors' coffee-klatch conversation that day.

Aunt Pauline was bigger than life everywhere, and Uncle Johnny accepted his role as her unseen and unheard mate. I do not remember Uncle Johnny ever saying anything except when we were by ourselves. And then he talked, bragged, boasted, exaggerated and amused the children.

The Most Important Man in Town

Burroughs, Georgia, was an important town, and my Uncle Johnny was the most important man in town. I say "town." Burroughs consisted of two houses on Uncle Johnny's side of the tracks and a store and two houses on the other side. Nothing else. No town hall, no fire station, but about 500 yards down the Atlantic Coastline tracks was that large potato warehouse revealing faded red paint peeling from the dilapidated building. The Atlantic Coastline Railroad company had painted the name "Burroughs" on the gable of the warehouse.

Two competing railway companies operated from Miami, Florida, to New York City, and the only place their tracks crossed was at Burroughs—at least that is what Uncle Johnny told me. I am not sure I trust everything he said. One set of tracks belonged to the Atlantic Coastline Railroad, and the other to the Seaboard Railroad.

Uncle Johnny worked at the intersection of these tracks in a tall tower consisting of windows on three sides so he could see trains coming from all directions. The tall tower looked like an airport tower, only not as tall. It was my Uncle Johnny's job to make sure the Seaboard train did not crash into an Atlantic Coastline train.

That made Uncle Johnny the most important man in town. To hear him talk when the ladies were not around, he held the destiny of hundreds in his hands. Uncle Johnny threw six-foot levers to stop trains, and pulled other levers to open switches. Before the days of electronic automation, that little bald-headed man had the strength to pull a lever and by a series of cables raise a flag that started or stopped a powerful locomotive a mile away. He also had the disposition to smile while he was doing it.

None of my uncles were as strong as Uncle Johnny, not even my daddy. They were all bigger, but I saw them strain at the giant, six-foot levers. Uncle Johnny jerked them into place and we all peered down the track to see a puff of smoke and blowing steam as a train labored to pull its load.

Uncle Johnny taught me that everybody wants to be somebody, and that we keep looking until we find that comfortable place in life. If you were married to Aunt Pauline, however, who could you be?

Overcoming Difficult Circumstances

I used to ask myself, *How did Aunt Pauline get weird?* I never admired her, but I liked her. I did not go to her house any more than I had to because it was so dirty. Once when my brother, Richard, was visiting her, she took a dirty plate off the table, wiped it with a napkin and said, "This is easier than washing."

Richard jumped up and said, "I love to wash dishes." He lied, but he thought lying was better than eating off someone else's dirty plate.

Uncle Johnny just rolled his eyes and chuckled. He did not approve, but what could he do?

When put in difficult circumstances, people seek level ground above sea level. Uncle Johnny found his perch in life among the boys and with the men.

Principles to Take Away

1. *The principle of abnormal normality.* Aunt Pauline was not mentally off, nor did she need institutionalization. She was odd, she did things differently, yet she liked people and thought people liked her. Aunt Pauline probably thought she was as normal as you and I think we are. In her abnormal way, she was very normal.
2. *The principle of found importance.* Uncle Johnny taught me that everyone finds self-importance one way or another. Because he could not get it at home, Uncle Johnny got his self-respect among children and at work.
3. *The principle of family toleration—and its limits.* My father and mother put up with Aunt Pauline, but only so far. They were nice to her as long as she did not cross certain boundaries.

"Learning not to quit too soon"

17

Uncle Johnny: Moving a Mountain-Boxcar

Uncle Johnny liked to show off in front of the kids. Although 11-year-old boys can often recognize when people are not speaking from the heart, I was never sure if Uncle Johnny was telling me the truth or just showing off.

One warm autumn day Uncle Johnny invited me to walk down the tracks to the potato warehouse on the Atlantic Coastline track siding. I was wearing a cream-colored windbreaker; he wore only a short-sleeved shirt. The chilly weather did not bother him.

As we walked the tracks, I wondered about the long steel pole he usually brought along to move empty boxcars. This time, however, he did not carry it with him.

"There was a lake about that big in France," Uncle Johnny said, pointing to a gigantic puddle of water flooding a potato field. "We saw the Germans on the other side of the water before they saw us."

Uncle Johnny described how he and a squad of American soldiers sneaked up to a German trench and killed the "Krauts" in a vicious cross fire before they could reach their rifles. I thought the story was fishy, even for my 11 years and lack of maturity. I was wise enough, though, not to mock him or question him.

"Yes, sir," I responded with a youthful nod of my head, as though the story convinced me. We reached the potato warehouse and I ran ahead to see how many potatoes filled each bin. Not that Uncle Johnny told me to check them; it was just my childish curiosity.

Moving an Empty Boxcar

"We gotta bring up an empty boxcar and put it in place for the workers tomorrow morning," Johnny yelled across the empty warehouse floor, his voice echoing off the open ceiling. Burroughs was too far from Savannah for the railroad to send a "switching" locomotive to push boxcars into place. It was the job of a man who carried a steel pole.

I had seen Uncle Johnny move boxcars by himself on several occasions. This small man could push a loaded boxcar down the track by using that long steel pole. It looked like a hoe handle with a small hook on one end. Uncle Johnny pried the hook between a wheel and the steel track, then using the enormous power of leverage, he could roll a loaded boxcar a few inches. He quickly jammed the steel hook under the wheel again before the car came to a full stop. Pressing down, he worked the hook between steel wheel and steel track, moving the boxcar out of the loading zone.

"Where's your steel pole?" I innocently asked the sly old fox.

"Don't need it," Uncle Johnny replied. Then he grinned, and his face crackled with impishness.

"Let's just push it," he said. "You and I can push it into place."

I thought he was kidding, but went along with the joke. I jumped off the warehouse platform onto the rocks of the railroad bed. Then, putting my shoulder to the faded red boxcar, I said jokingly, "Sure. We can move it." I did not mean it, and I knew Uncle Johnny knew I did not mean it. He knew I could not move the boxcar, so it was a childish gesture to try. When two people say something they both know the other person knows is not meant, however, they begin to share the truth.

Seeing with the Eye of an Ant

"Something you need to learn from the eye of an ant," Uncle Johnny told me. "Every time you lean against something, it moves," he explained. Then he jumped down on the tracks, placed one hand against the red boxcar and pushed slightly.

Uncle Johnny explained that every action produces a reaction. "If you jump up and down on the ground, you'll wobble this planet in its orbit," he said.

"You didn't see that heavy boxcar move because you're too big," Uncle Johnny continued to analyze. "But an ant on the track could see it move because it's right down where the steel wheel touches the steel track."

Standing at the end of that boxcar, Uncle Johnny explained that every action produces a reaction. He pointed out how small I was. "But if you jump up and down on the ground, you'll wobble this planet in its orbit," he said.

I believed Uncle Johnny, and in a childish reaction I jumped up and down a few times. This was the uncle I had just doubted killed Germans, yet I believed the planet had just wobbled under my jump.

"Now let's move this boxcar!" Uncle Johnny said, grinning at me. "Put your shoulder on the car and your feet on the cross tie."

He explained that I should not just use my arm muscles to push because I would wear out. He told me to use my leg power, and lean against the train.

"Pretend like you're leaning against a wall to hold it up."

I obeyed, leaning all 73 pounds of my body weight against the boxcar.

"Don't push too hard or you'll get tired and quit," Uncle Johnny advised. Then he leaned next to me and we both put our feet on the cross ties and settled in for a long exercise.

"It's already started to move," Uncle Johnny said softly so as not to use too much energy talking. "Just keep pushin'..." We talked and leaned for a long time; I do not remember how long. Time creeps slowly for little boys who are in a hurry to do everything.

"Keep the pressure constant," Uncle Johnny warned. "If it stops, we'll have to work hard to get it rolling again."

"My foot is slipping," I whispered to Uncle Johnny.

"Keep pushing," he grunted.

But my foot is slipping, I thought quietly, but did not say anything. Then it occurred to me that it seemed a little longer than before from the cross tie to the boxcar. I felt as though I was having to stretch farther to keep pushing. I did not want to say anything because I was not sure if Uncle Johnny was "pulling my leg." He could be telling me a fib to make me look stupid. If I said we were moving when we were not, he would have a good laugh at my expense.

Slowly Seeing Results

So I said nothing. I leaned my head against the wooden frame of the boxcar and spotted a line from my eye to the edge of the boxcar to a place on the ground. I chose a black mark on a granite chip.

Sure enough, the chip moved away from my focus. That meant the boxcar car was moving! I wanted to yell out that we did it, but I was afraid of Uncle Johnny's ridicule. I did not want him to laugh at me, and I knew he would tell the rest of the family and they would laugh, too.

I lined up my eyes with another rock off the edge of the boxcar. Uncle Johnny said something, but I did not want to talk. I wanted to find out if we were moving. *Don't talk,* I thought, and I gave the boxcar an extra push. When the second rock moved beyond the line of my eye, I knew we were moving.

"We're moving," I said, but calmly, almost as if it were a question. You would think I would have laughed or yelled, but I was still afraid Uncle Johnny was somehow pulling a trick on me.

Look for Little Evidences of Progress

To this day, I don't get overly excited—at least I don't show it outwardly. Inwardly I can be ecstatic. The greatest occurrences in my life may cause me to smile inwardly, or to feel a surge of confidence, but they usually don't get a shout from me. When I know I am right, or I have made it work, or when I have done something no one else has done, I may laugh to show some emotion, but I do a good job of controlling it. I do not know if that is the way I was born, or if it is something I have learned from people such as Uncle Johnny. But it is me.

That memorable Sunday afternoon, Uncle Johnny and I moved the empty boxcar maybe one or two feet. I do not know how far, but that is not important. I know we moved it. We pushed it—a small man in his 50s and a young boy.

Today when I am working on an "impossible" task, I remember moving that boxcar. These were important lessons. Don't quit too soon; keep pushing even if you think nothing is happening; don't give in to your feelings; look for little evidences of progress; don't get discouraged.

I have written several books of more than a thousand pages—a formidable task for a writer. I tell myself I can write a 365-page book in a year if I write a page a day. Do a little every day; don't quit; ignore your discouragement; watch for little evidences of progress.

Principles to Take Away

1. *The inward smile principle.* I learned not to cheer an accomplishment too soon lest I embarrass myself by claiming something that did not happen. On the other hand, I learned that others do not appreciate your applauding yourself too late after a personal achievement. So the best thing to do is just to smile inwardly and know that you have done a good job. That is the most satisfying applause of all.

2. *The "timing of victory" principle.* It is hard to know when to claim victory in life. Life's movement can be similar to that of a boxcar being pushed by an older man and a young kid. When do we know we have done it? Take victory as it comes in each module of time.

3. *The principle of unperceived movement.* Moving the boxcar taught me that when I exert force, things are happening

that I can't always see. I must keep pushing by faith even when I can't see results.

4. *The principle of taking joy from small progress.* When I was pushing the boxcar, I wanted to give up at first because I did not immediately see results. When I could empirically see the results of my work, however, I took heart and continued to push.

5. *The principle of moving the immovable.* Often we can't move the things in life we think are immovable because we never start. Moving an immovable object takes (a) a beginning, (b) energy, (c) constant pressure and (d) inner determination.

6. *The principle of experienced encouragement.* We will not do most things in life without encouragement from older, wiser and more experienced counsel. When someone tells you it has been done before, it is easier to think we can do it too.

Part V

---·—·—·—·—·—·—·—·—·—·—·—·—·—·—·—·---

Doing Wrong, Naturally

No one has to teach us to lie or be mischievous or fail. We all have a dark and a bright side of our natures. I learned early that everyone is Dr. Jekyll and Mr. Hyde, Beauty and the Beast. Why did I do wrong? As the song suggests, I was "doing what comes naturally."

My mother and teachers gave me lofty ideals and, at times, unrealistic dreams. They gave me visions they never achieved and standards by which they never lived. Some of my failures were the result of dreaming "the impossible dream."

My boyish waywardness, however, turned into some fortunate lessons. I learned early that sin is a bitter taskmaster, much harsher than trying to live a good life. I learned to find happiness in obedience, and discovered that obeying is more enjoyable than doing wrong.

"Stealing brought me no satisfaction—1941"

18

Bellyacher: No Enjoyment in a Stolen Dream

I remember the first thing I ever intentionally stole. It was a little toy lead soldier from Handy Andy's Variety Store on the corner of Anderson and Waters Avenue in Savannah, when I was in the third grade. World War II had just started, and the patriotic thing to do was to support our soldiers, write letters to our older cousins overseas and buy war bonds. When we had a chance, we played with toy soldiers.

My next-door neighbor, Shirley Hoffman, always had money to buy toy lead soldiers. I had very little money for toys. We rented our house from the Hoffmans, and the fact that they owned two houses meant they were much richer than we were. Before the days of toy plastic soldiers, the only ones available were lead soldiers. I owned maybe three or four that I kept in a cardboard box, but they were not up-to-date soldiers. Mine wore World War I helmets, whereas the new 1941 models sported World War II helmets. Shirley Hoffman owned more than two dozen up-to-date, lead toy soldiers.

When Shirley Hoffman and I played war, her Bellyacher could spray machine-gun fire and keep my soldiers who were holding rifles from attacking. So I rationalized, I need a Bellyacher.

Handy Andy's Variety Store sold the toy lead soldiers for a nickel apiece. The one I wanted more than anything else, however, cost 15 cents. Shirley Hoffman owned a soldier like the one I wanted the most. I called this toy lead soldier "Bellyacher" because he was lying on his stomach, shooting a machine gun. I assumed anyone who lay on his stomach that long would have an ache in his belly. Several of these toy lead Bellyachers were in stock at Handy Andy's Variety Store, and I just had to have one.

When Shirley Hoffman and I played war, she lined up her toy lead soldiers with rifles against my toy lead soldiers with rifles. Then her Bellyacher could spray machine-gun fire across the field of action. According to our rules of war, her machine-gun fire kept my soldiers who were holding rifles from attacking. So I rationalized, *I need a Bellyacher.*

Conceiving the Great Toy Robbery

Handy Andy's Variety Store was about a half block out of my way when I walked home from school each evening. For about a week, I went into the store just to look at the toy lead soldiers and dream about Bellyacher. While I was dreaming about the toy lead soldiers I conceived of the "great toy robbery."

I noticed that the clerk sitting near the front door paid little attention to me as I lusted for the toy lead soldiers. She usually just read a magazine. I sat in school and thought how easy it would be to take a toy lead soldier and slip it into my pocket, then walk casually out the front door. Although the clerk usually saw me in the store, she knew I did not have any money; so she would not expect anything if I walked out, as I had done so many times before. For a third grader, the plan was brilliantly conceived. Then again, I wanted a practice run.

A Practice Run
So one day I went the half block out of my way, and walked into Handy Andy's Variety Store.

"Hi," I said with wide-eyed naiveté. "Isn't it a beautiful day?"

"Huh," the clerk groaned without looking up from her magazine.

I walked to the back of Handy Andy's Variety Store and began handling the various toy lead soldiers. Glancing up to the front, I saw that the clerk was still reading. I must have been guilt-ridden because I did not put Bellyacher in my pocket for the practice run. I just took a nickel rifleman and put him in my pocket. I began to walk toward the door.

"You want something?" The clerk spoke to me.

"No ma'am."

She looked at me until another customer came in. I had rationalized that if I put another rifleman into my pocket, not Bellyacher, then I was not guilty of what I intended to do. When the clerk was not looking, I slipped the rifleman out of my pocket, played with him a few minutes and put him back on the counter.

"So long...I'll see ya tomorrow," I said, leaving the store.

A Commitment to the Crime
The next day in school I did not learn anything about reading, writing and arithmetic. All day long I reviewed my strategy, again and again, plotting how I would do it. My "great toy robbery" was so well-thought through, I was convinced nothing could go wrong.

Right after school let out, I walked straight to Handy Andy's Variety Store. The closer I came to the store, the harder my heart beat. I felt the weight of every Sunday School lesson I had ever heard. I wanted to turn and run for home, but I couldn't. I had made such a deep commitment to the crime that stealing Bellyacher had become a matter of principle. I even rationalized that stealing it was a matter of character. Because I had told myself I was going to do it and had spent so much time planning the "great toy robbery," backing out would constitute a character flaw. I asked myself, "Are you man enough to do what you promised you would do?"

"Hi," I said to the magazine-reading clerk. "It sure is a beautiful day."

"Yep," she said without looking up.

I had planned to spend the usual amount of time in the back of the store, just as on any other day. I had rationalized that if I walked in and out, my hurried exit might arouse suspicion. So when I got to the back of the store I began to play with the lead toy soldiers.

I had to go to the bathroom and it was a long way to the field where we boys "went" behind a convenient tree. The pressure of guilt not only made my heart race, but it also weighed heavily on my bladder.

"Wow," I said under my breath. I saw two new machine gunners. These were bigger toy lead soldiers carrying bigger machine guns. Now I was confused by the options. The bigger machine gunner was sitting down firing a .50-caliber machine gun, and a second soldier was cast in the same dye. The second soldier was feeding ammunition into the machine gun; but it was still just 15 cents. Just think—two soldiers for the price of one!

Another new soldier was like the first, sitting down firing a .50-caliber machine gun, but he was behind a stone wall and no one was feeding ammunition into his gun.

I played with the two new soldiers for a while, thinking how effectively they would keep Shirley Hoffman's soldiers from attacking me. I thought that the two-soldier machine gun might be better in battle. If one of the soldiers got killed, the second could carry on the machine-gun fire. So I almost decided to steal the two-soldier machine gun instead of the Bellyacher I had planned to steal.

Then I began to think. *Do what you came to do,* I told myself. *You have always wanted Bellyacher. Now you'd better get him.*

Just about the time I was ready to pocket the Bellyacher, two ladies came into the store. They shopped their way toward the back, looking at various counters. I was getting antsy and impatient. I had to go to the bathroom and it was a long way to the field where we boys "went" behind a convenient tree. The pressure of guilt not only made my heart race, but it also weighed heavily on my bladder.

Then the moment came. The two ladies were behind me, their backs turned. They were looking at items in the fingernail-polish section. I quickly glanced toward the front. The clerk was still reading her magazine. My eyes darted back and forth, and as slick as a third-grade boy could do it, Bellyacher disappeared from the counter and into my pocket.

I slowly walked toward the clerk, looking at the various items on the counter. I tried to be as nonchalant as a lady who is shopping. I picked up one item, put it back, then another. Then I heard her from up front. "Don't touch the lipstick," the clerk told me.

"I'm sorry..."

"Don't touch anything you're not going to buy," she said, never looking up from her magazine as she talked. "Except the toys," she said, still not looking at me. "You can play with the toys. Only put them back when you're finished."

Did she know? I frantically asked myself. *Did she see me pick up Bellyacher?* Because she saw me pick up the lipstick, but never looked up, could she see me pick up Bellyacher?

It was too late to go back and return the lead toy soldier, although I was fearful she might grab me as I went by. Worse than that, she might tell the teachers at school; or the worst scenario ever, tell my mother. Not knowing what to do, I continued to smile, and I continued to walk. When I pushed the door to go out, the little bell tinkled.

"See ya tomorrow," I said.

I was on the outside. I had committed the crime. Bellyacher was in my pocket.

Don't look back, I told myself. I walked down Waters Avenue away from Anderson Street and never looked back. Continuing to walk for about five blocks, I could not wait to reach the tree in the field. I turned into an alley, and in an empty garage I did what my bladder told me to do.

The Sergeant Was Coming to Get Me

After walking through Live Oak Park, I started through the empty field where our special tree was located. That's when I saw him coming. Sergeant Sullivan was cruising toward me in a black, 1939 Chevy County Police cruiser. A chrome-plated siren was mounted on the left front fender. It was not screaming, but I panicked anyway. I knew in my heart he was coming for me. My legs were water. I knew I could not outrun the cruiser. Even if I could, Sergeant Sullivan knew where I lived.

I thought back to the clerk at Handy Andy's. She called the police! Sergeant Sullivan was coming to get me!

My first thought was to slip Bellyacher out of my pocket and drop it into the tall grass. That way, when Sergeant Sullivan frisked me, he would not find the stolen toy. Then I remembered seeing a

This was it. I dropped my books and threw both hands in the air, surrendering to Sergeant Sullivan as though I were a bank robber.

movie about a crook who dropped the stolen item, but the police retraced his steps and found it.

So I did not drop Bellyacher.

I began to think of excuses and lies, anything to get out of my mess.

I could say I had been playing with Bellyacher and forgot I had it in my pocket.

The lie began to grow. I had three or four lead toy soldiers in my hand, I could say. I put them all back but one, and forgot he was in my pocket.

That was what I was going to tell Sergeant Sullivan after he frisked me and found the stolen merchandise. When the cruiser came closer, I saw another county patrolman sitting with him in the 1939 Chevy sedan.

This was worse than I expected. They sent two men out to get me.

As they approached from Cedar Street, Sergeant Sullivan threw up his big left hand out the window in my direction.

This was it. I dropped my books and threw both hands in the air, surrendering to Sergeant Sullivan as though I were a bank robber.

Then he waved, and the other officer also waved. They were just waving! They were just being friendly. I smiled, and tried to turn my surrender into a wave; it was halfhearted and clumsy.

To this day I wonder what Sergeant Sullivan thought of a young kid who threw up both hands to surrender when he drove by. Did he think I was being sarcastic, the way some modern-day kids might put down a police officer?

After Sergeant Sullivan passed, I looked back at every corner to see if he was coming after me. If God had a sense of humor, He could have sent a fire truck or ambulance into the neighborhood with siren blaring and I would have died of guilt in the third grade. But nothing like that happened. God had a better plan to stop a budding thief.

Hiding the Evidence

When I arrived home, it dawned on me that I could not take Bellyacher into the house. Mother might ask where I got the toy lead soldier. Because I did not have money to buy a soldier, she would have surely suspected I stole it. Although I was not smart enough to think of every angle, I was smart enough to realize that my mother was much smarter than I was. If she saw a new soldier, she would surely suspect something and ask about it.

I went around to the north side of the house, the side where no one ever went, and crawled under the house. There I hid Bellyacher in the floor joists. After all, I had seen my father hide his liquor bottles there to keep them from my mother. Why couldn't I do the same?

Next came the hardest punishment of all. Shirley Hoffman came over to play toy soldiers. She brought her wooden box and two dozen toy lead soldiers. She arranged a skirmish line and positioned her Bellyacher machine gunner off to the right. I set out my skirmish line of World War I soldiers wearing their old-fashioned helmets. I did not have a Bellyacher to lay down a field of machine-gun fire. At least I did not have a Bellyacher to show Shirley Hoffman. While we were playing, my Bellyacher had to stay in his hiding place under the house. I could not tell Shirley Hoffman I had a Bellyacher because she might have told my mother.

Never before had I hated playing toy soldiers as I hated playing that afternoon. Outwardly I continued playing, but inwardly I was crushed. I felt guilty because I had stolen Bellyacher, yet I was envious to show him off to Shirley Hoffman.

God's Effective Punishment

That night, guilt kept me awake. I listened for the wail of a siren in the darkness. I worried. I was too embarrassed to tell Mother what I did. So that night in bed I decided I could never play with Bellyacher. I experienced one of this life's most severe punishments—to gain your heart's desire and not be able to use it, to enjoy it or to ever share it with anybody.

Growing up, I forgot about Bellyacher until after my conversion. I never went back to get him. I left my toy lead soldier in the floor joists of the house at 107 Wagner Street. I did not go back to confess to the owners of Handy Andy's Variety Store, nor did I ever make restoration. God knows I am sorry. He also effectively stopped me from shop-lifting in the future through the incident with Bellyacher.

When I was old enough to go back and look under the floor joist to see if my toy lead soldier was still there, the house was gone. An expressway had been built right through the former location of the front door, and Habitat for Humanity had moved the house and refurbished it for a needy family.

--- --- --- --- --- --- --- --- --- --- --- ---

Principles to Take Away

--- --- --- --- --- --- --- --- --- --- --- ---

1. *The principle of total depravity.* I learned that there was a dark side to my personality even as a child. I lied and stole to get the things I wanted while appearing to be a "nice" child. I was deceptive. If I could do it, so could other children, and my children and grandchildren.

2. *The principle of a guilty conscience.* When I stole the toy, I experienced guilt and agony. My conviction was more disastrous to my feelings than was my anticipated joy in hav-

ing a soldier. I am thankful for a conscience because it kept me (as it keeps others) from a destructive life.

3. *The principle of lust.* I learned early that powerful appetites within me could drive me to do things contrary to my rearing. Yet when I gave in to my lust, I did not derive the satisfaction it promised me.

4. *The principle of unusable loot.* After I had gone through the agonizing experience of stealing a toy, I never had the satisfaction of playing with it.

19

Cussing: Struggling to Quit

I began to curse in the fourth grade. I still remember the event that triggered it, and the person involved. We were in Mrs. Baxley's class on the second floor of Waters Avenue School. A short guy who had dark brown curly hair and was wearing glasses—I forget his name—sat behind me.

Instead of reading the assigned paper at my desk, I had turned around in my seat and was whispering to the short guy behind me. What we were whispering about is inconsequential. He secretly slipped a hand-drawn picture to me.

"See?" he whispered.

He giggled quietly, pointing at a word on his paper. He had drawn a house and a family of stick figures. The size of the stick figures revealed two children. The father was taller than the mother, and the balloon coming out of the father's mouth contained a crudely printed curse word.

"D_____," my buddy whispered, and laughed again. "That's what grown men say." Then he said it again: "D_____."

I knew the word. My uncles used it. Not around women and children, but I overheard it. Ladies and children did not curse. My Sunday School teacher had told me not to curse. I had memorized the commandment, "Thou shalt not take the name of the Lord thy God in vain" (Exod. 20:7, *KJV*). I knew the *D* word was wrong, too.

"D_____," my buddy said yet again, still chuckling.

"Don't say that," I whispered, with the innocence of a fourth grader.

"What's wrong with d____?" he asked. His father used the word, he said. And I knew that my father used the word.

"Come on," he coaxed. "Everybody says it when they get big." As it was for many kids, cursing for him was a sign of growing up.

I Was a Fast Learner

I quietly repeated the cuss word in my mind. I felt a warm emotion trickle out of my brain. I had just said the word silently, not out loud. Sure enough—it made me feel big and grown up. I was doing something that made me one of the guys. A slow smile turned the corners of my mouth upward. Again I repeated the word silently. Rather than feeling convicted, or bad, I felt affirmed.

My mouth formed the word "d____," but no sound came out.

"Yeah" said my buddy, encouragingly: "D____."

Then I said it out loud.

Angels did not swoop down to hit me, and my mouth did not get lockjaw. Instead of feeling bad, I felt good.

My buddy and I went out for recess. I was eager to try out my new vocabulary on the playground. I looked for a place I could use my newly acquired skill. Finally the opportunity came. I remember exactly what I said. We were playing cops and robbers. I bumped into someone and yelled, "Get out of the d____ way," but got caught anyway.

A couple of guys stopped and looked at me. I could tell they were surprised. We had all heard cursing, but they had not heard me do it. Instead of feeling big, I felt small the way they looked at me. They were shocked that I cursed, and cursed one of them. I felt self-conscious. Then I was scared they might tell Mother; I knew what that meant—a whipping.

Instead of saying I was sorry, I repeated the word again. I was showing off, trying to be a big shot, trying to recapture the good feeling I had when I first used the word.

"I always say that," I boasted as I lied.

During the next year or two I continued to curse, as did all my buddies in the Cat Patrol. We were careful not to curse around our

---

Among the Cat Patrol, I was not the most prolific curser. Bobby Arnold took that prize. I did not have the cleanest mouth, either. One of the other boys took that prize.

---

mothers and other women, and around teachers, but only around each other.

My vocabulary grew as I heard other words and mastered them, too. My Sunday School training kept me from using God's name in vain, however, or blaspheming the name of Jesus Christ.

If Mother or Daddy ever overheard me cursing, they did not say anything; and I never remember getting a whipping for cursing. Among the Cat Patrol, I was not the most prolific curser. Bobby Arnold took that prize. I did not have the cleanest mouth, either. One of the other boys took that prize.

Burning My Filthy Words

I tried to quit cursing when I started attending Presbyterian Youth Fellowship (PYF). The young people of Eastern Heights Presbyterian Church met for PYF on Sunday evening at about six o'clock in an upstairs assembly room. One of the ladies played the piano and we sang hymns.

Everyone read a part out of a book in the PYF meeting. We had only one PYF book. Usually, one of the ladies read the introduction that explained the theme for the evening. Then the book, which was really a magazine, was passed from youth to youth. Each one read his or her part aloud. I did not look forward to reading aloud because I did not read well in public.

One evening, the material in the book asked us to make a promise to God. As we read the various parts in the book, we were asked to quit a sin. Cursing was one of the sins mentioned, but I did not read that part. Someone else read the part that warned, "God will not hold the person guiltless who takes God's name in vain."

I felt conviction because I knew some of my words were wrong. I did not say anything out loud at the PYF meeting, but in my heart I knew cursing was wrong. The PYF book offered a prayer for us and I prayed it with the others.

"Lord forgive me of my sin," I prayed, and I meant it. Then I added, "My sin is cursing."

All the young people at that PYF meeting did something to seal our pledges. I don't know whether it was suggested in the PYF book or if one of the ladies thought of it, but it was something we did several times. One of the ladies lit a candle on the small table in front of the young people. About 10 or 11 of us were present. We were told the flame of the candle stood for purity. It was burning away filth and impurity.

Next we were given little slips of paper and a small church pencil. (I call a church pencil one that is not quite long enough to hold in your hand.) The lady waited until we had all received pencil and paper. "Write your sin on that piece of paper," she ordered, in apostolic authority. "Whatever you do that's wrong, just write it on the paper." She explained that no one would see what we wrote because the slips of paper would be burned. We were to place the slips of paper in the metal pan on the table.

I did not want anyone to see what I wrote. At church I was ashamed of my cursing. None of the Cat Patrol attended Eastern Heights Presbyterian Church so they could not tell on me. And I surely did not curse around the church.

I stretched my slip of paper on my knee and cupped my hand around what I was writing so no one could see. Then I printed carefully: Cussing. I folded the paper quickly so no one could see what I wrote. I dropped it into the pan and waited.

We bowed our heads in prayer. Then the lady took the candle

and torched the slips of paper. First one caught fire, then another. They burned slowly.

There they go, God, I thought. *There goes my sin up in smoke.*

I fully expected that event to rid me of my habit of cursing. I rode home in the backseat of Rev. Williams's car, thinking deep theological thoughts. I thought I had done a great religious act. I thought God had thrust that candle into my chest cavity and burned out all my cursing. I had been asked by the ladies to surrender to God, and I had done it.

Disillusioned at Cursing Again

Later that week, in a fit of anger, I cursed with the Cat Patrol. We were sitting around somewhere and one of the guys cursed something and the other guys said, "Yeah," and they cursed.

Then I cursed, too.

I was disillusioned. I expected God to keep my mouth clean, but a filthy word came out. Sometimes when I cursed I felt good. This time I felt dirty. I felt like one of the guys, but inwardly I did not want to curse.

"It was just a slip," I told myself, justifying what just happened. "But I won't do it again."

The cursing, though, happened again, and again, and again. The commitment to stop cursing was not accompanied with the deep emotional movement of a committed will. So it was easy to do what the other guys did—I cursed.

Yet I did not see myself as a curser.

Confessing and Burning Each Cuss Word

A second consecration service took place at PYF, again including the candle, short pencils and tin pan. I attended the Sunday evening service and we again sang hymns as the lady played the piano. We again read out of the PYF book as it was passed from youth to youth. Then the candle was lit on the table. Slips of paper were passed to each of us again, along with the short stubby pencils.

Didn't work last time, I told myself.

This time, however, it would be different. This time I would be more sincere.

"Write your sins on the slip of paper," we were told. "The fire will stand for cleansing."

I held a hymnbook on my lap, and again I cupped my hand around my slip of paper so no one could see what I was about to reveal. The last time I had written the descriptive word "cussing." But it had not worked; I went back to foul language. This time I decided to write the words I said. In my childish way I thought that if I wrote out each word, the words themselves would go up in smoke. *The fire will burn them out of my mind*, I said to myself.

I gazed intently as the candle touched the pieces of paper. "This time I mean business," I prayed to God. I had a glint in my eye and a tightening of the lips. After all, I thought, I confessed each cuss word, writing them out one by one.

I began to write small—very small—because I knew a lot of words. I did not have any trouble with the four-letter words—they came easy. Most of the exotic words though were longer, and I could not spell them. I have never been a good speller. Apparently, I was taking too long.

The lady said, "Elmer, what are you writing?"

Quickly I put both hands over my paper. I sure did not want anyone to see what I had written. I was in church.

I folded my paper filled with written filthy words. I was careful not to include religious words of blasphemy on my list. I could never bear to write those words.

I gazed intently as the candle touched the pieces of paper in the pan. "This time I mean business," I prayed to God. I had a glint in my eye and a tightening of the lips. I vowed not to slip. *After all, I thought, I confessed each cuss word, writing them out one by one.*

Giving Up on Cleaning My Mouth

Within two weeks I cursed again. Because this was the second time I had promised and the second time I had fallen, it did not make such an impression on me, so I don't remember the circumstances. All I remember was that I gave up trying to clean my mouth.

I cursed freely with the Cat Patrol again. Although we were not as filthy as some youth today, we were not angels. We cussed in anger. We cussed to boast. We cussed in frustration, and we cussed to be one of the boys.

Each Sunday School lesson or sermon that mentioned cursing caused me to be progressively less convicted. I could read the Ten Commandments and not be affected when I repeated, "Thou shalt not take the name of the Lord thy God in vain" (Exod. 20:7, *KJV*).

The Eloquent Campfire Confession

I went to Camp Laurel Walker with the Presbyterians each summer, beginning when I was 11. Camp was a great experience for me. Each year on the last night of camp we rededicated ourselves to God at a campfire service.

I made a big display at the campfire service involving my cursing when I was 13. Dr. Charles Woodbridge was my cabin counselor and the speaker that week. His Ph.D. from the University of Berlin, Germany, impressed me. His messages were funny, interesting and Bible based.

The campfire was built down near the lake, in front of the amphitheater. The fire was lit and we sang gospel choruses. Dr. Woodbridge delivered a message from the Bible.

Then it was time for testimonies. One by one my buddies went forward, took a small stick or wood chip and threw it into the fire. It was supposed to mean they were becoming a part of the flame that would light the world for Jesus.

One by one my buddies told how much they learned from the Bible classes or from the sermons. They said how much they liked the food, or they expressed appreciation for their friends. Most of them pledged their love to Christ and told how they planned to serve Him.

I had been convicted of my filthy mouth. I knew the campfire service was where decisions were made for God. People were changed at campfire. People were saved at Friday night campfire.

I confidently strolled to the front and picked up a wood chip about as long as a man's hand. It was the kind of chip that split off when a sharp ax cut soundly into a tree.

"See this chip?" I announced to the campers, holding it up for all to see. "My tongue is as dirty as this chip." The pine chip was once a clean, pale yellow, but the rain had splattered it with black mud.

"Just like this chip has mud on it, my tongue is coated with filthy cussing." I honestly don't know where I acquired the eloquence. Although I was sincere before God in what I said to them, I had a lot of pride in me that evening.

"I want God to cleanse me from cussing," I told the group. The lessons of the candle burning the slips of paper in the metal pan had not been forgotten.

"For to me, to live is Christ," I testified from Philippians 1:21. I said several other things and pledged myself in front of my friends to serve Christ. Then, dramatically, I threw the chip into the fire, saying, "I join all of you in being a light for Christ."

Cussing Again—On the Church Steps

I returned home and kept my promise for about a month and a half, not cussing once. It was easier to keep my promise because I was no longer in junior high school and my friend was Arthur Winn. The boys of the Cat Patrol began moving away from Wagner Heights, and I was running around with Arthur. We did not cuss too much, only once in a while. Arthur had been at the campfire and heard my promise. So I was not tempted to cuss around Arthur, and he did not cuss around me—very much.

I was delivering the *Savannah Evening Press* and Arthur helped me with the paper route. I picked up my papers in front of Morningside Baptist Church, and when it rained, Pastor Cecil Underwood allowed us to fold them on the front porch of the church. The papers came in stacks of 100 each, tied with wire. I usually grabbed the wire with my bare hands and bent it back and forth about 50 times until the wire broke. Breaking the wire was a daily ritual. When the papers came this particular day, I vigorously began bending the wire on one stack back and forth. Suddenly it broke, much more quickly than I expected, cutting my knuckle.

"Oh d____!" I cursed.

"You promised you weren't going to cuss," Arthur scolded me in a tutorial voice.

"Oh d____ you!" I said. I was mad, and I directed my venom at him.

"You're cussing on the church steps," he rebuked me.

"Oh d____ the church!" I exclaimed. I blush today at what I said back then.

The cut on my thumb was so deep that I have a scar till this day. I was mad and cursed the wire, the paper route, and anything and anyone I could think of. I let it all hang out. After that I continued to curse casually around Arthur, but not as bad as I did that afternoon.

The story, however, has a deeper conclusion.

Accepting Christ Cured the Cussing

"I can't quit cursing," I told myself. I had honestly tried to stop, but each time I slipped back into my old habit. From that experience on

---

I really thought a filthy mouth came from hearing other people curse or seeing profanity, such as that on a rest room wall. I was wrong. Cursing comes from the human heart.

---

the church porch until I was converted, I continued to curse casually. I did not try to quit again. I had given it my best shot, but could not conquer a filthy mouth.

I once told myself that I cursed because of the rest room walls of the world. Every time I went into a men's rest room, I saw words that triggered a reaction.

I wish there were one eraser big enough to clean every rest room wall, I once thought. Then I concluded, *And big enough to erase my mind and the thoughts of everyone else in the world.* I really thought a filthy mouth came from hearing other people curse or seeing profanity, such as that on a rest room wall. I was wrong. Cursing comes from the human heart. You can get rid of cursing or any other sin when you acquire a new heart.

I was converted on July 25, 1950. Cursing was not an issue of my salvation. When I was converted I did not repent specifically of cursing, or tell God I was sorry for my foul mouth. I knew I was a sinner and that my whole life was filled with sin. I repented of sin. I asked Christ to come into my heart and He did. The presence of Jesus Christ in my life cleansed my mouth.

I did not say one curse word for 43 years. I have often testified at youth meetings or when preaching that I have not cursed since I was saved. Furthermore, I have never even thought curse words.

Perhaps my testimony was partly based on pride, but whatever its basis I can no longer say I have not cursed since I was saved in 1950. I let one more word slip. Perhaps God allowed it to humble me so I could no longer take pride in my testimony.

A Cure for Idle Boasting

It happened about 1993. I was speaking to about 100 people in a minister's Christian Education seminar. I think it was on the West Coast. Right in the middle of a sentence, a curse word came out of my mouth. It did not even fit the syntax of the sentence. Out of nowhere I said a curse word. My face flushed and I tried to go on speaking. I probably tried to act as though I had not cursed, but I had.

"Did you just hear me say a curse word?" I asked the shocked audience.

They shook their heads in the affirmative. Some spoke out, "Yes!"

"I've never cursed since I've been saved," I told them. "Not once." I was not sure they believed me; but I told them the story of the PYF and the candle that supposedly burned out my sin of cursing. I told them about the campfire. I told them I had not said a curse word since I was saved. "I no longer even think curse words," I said. "I don't have to struggle to keep my mind and mouth clean."

I explained to them that using the curse word had been an involuntary reaction. I said I know God did not put the word in my mouth. "For all I know, a demon could have put it there," I said. I don't emphasize spiritual warfare the way some Christians do, seeing a demon behind every problem and temptation. I think most of our sin problems come from our own lust. I am not, however, naive about spiritual warfare. I know we "wrestle against principalities and powers in high places." I think a dark angel could put such a word in a person's mouth.

"Let's stop and pray," I told the ministers. I prayed to ask forgiveness for the word I had said. I asked God for the cleansing of the blood, but more importantly, for the power of the blood to keep me from sin, both voluntary and involuntary.

"Send guardian angels to protect me," I prayed.

I have not thought or said a curse word since that experience, nor have I had to struggle to hold back such words. The experience has made me more sympathetic toward those who struggle with cursing. It has also kept me from idle boasting that I have not cursed since I was saved.

Principles to Take Away

1. *The principle of sin's immediate satisfaction.* I was immediately enticed and exhilarated by saying a curse word. I found fun in rebellion; but I was confused when my friends did not understand my newfound freedom from cursing.
2. *The principle of sin's external power.* Yes, sin is an action, a habit and an outward rebellion. I learned early, however, that external power can bring sin into a child's life. It can capture a child from without, and his or her inward desire to be free is too weak to resist. I struggled to overcome an outward power, and could only do it through another power—Christ.
3. *The principle of limitations of self-determination.* Mother had taught me that "A Towns can do anything." I could not break the habit of cursing by self-reformation alone, however, no matter how hard I tried.

"I only fooled myself when I lied—1939"

20

Slaw: The First Lie I Remember Telling

Although the psalmist said he was hasty in saying, "All men are liars" (Ps. 116:11), he would have had reason to draw that conclusion if he knew little boys such as Elmer Towns, Jr.

The Slaw Incident

I told the first lie I can remember when I was in the second grade. Notice, I said the first lie I *remember*. I probably exaggerated, denied or avoided the truth many times before the second grade. "The slaw incident," however, involved the first time I can remember telling a straightforward intentional untruth.

As I have said, I attended Waters Avenue School. A housing project was located nearby, in which lived a lot of kids whose parents worked in the shipyards during the years World War II was raging. These parents were not home to cook hot meals, so a federal government-subsidized hot-meal program came to Waters Avenue School.

I remember the first day I lined up to march single file into the basement for lunch. There it was—a sparkling, stainless-steel steam table. Spread out before me were large flat pans of food, each a different color.

"What's that, Ma'am?" I respectfully asked a cafeteria worker.

"Beets," was her abrupt reply.

"Don't put any beets on my plate," I said. "My momma don't cook beets." My plea did no good. A big spoonful of that dark red-root vegetable called "beets" was plopped onto my plate. Today if the school insists that kids eat stuff they don't want to, the children can hide behind their civil rights. That was not possible at Waters Avenue School—vegetables were a must.

When I tried to get away with not eating what they put on my plate, I was told, "If you don't clean your plate, you can't go out to play at recess." And they meant it. A large cafeteria attendant in a white uniform stood beside the garbage can into which we scraped our plates.

"No eat, no play," she said. So I choked down my beets.

The next day they served turnips, and I had to gag them down, too.

The next day something else was served that was no doubt good for us, but that many little boys did not like. This is where my first remembered lie came in.

Raw Shredded Cabbage in My Pocket

What they gave us was raw cabbage, sliced in shreds. That is all. Raw shredded cabbage. It was probably supposed to be slaw, but the juice was missing.

Dry shredded raw cabbage! The guys who had already eaten lunch had gone outside. They were playing a game I could hardly wait to play—probably cops and robbers.

"Uggggh!" I choked. The raw cabbage did not go down my throat. I drank some water and tried to swallow the cabbage again, but the large shreds caught in my throat and I choked. It came up and I spit the raw cabbage into my napkin. I was not playacting. I had tears in my eyes and, of course, I did not want anyone to see them. So I knotted up the raw cabbage in my napkin and pushed it under the edge of my plate. That is where the lie began.

"What's this slaw doing in your pocket?" Mother asked. I was caught. Then I said with all the calmness I could muster, "It was so good, I took extra to eat on the playground."

I thought about chewing up the rest of the cabbage on my plate and hiding it in my napkin, too, but too much cabbage still remained.

I looked to the left, and no one was watching. I turned to the right; no one was there either. I slowly reached my hand onto my plate and covered it with my other free hand. I fielded the whole pile of raw cabbage like a ground ball, and slickly pulled it into my lap. So far, so good.

Continuing the subterfuge, I filled my pocket with the cabbage. Again I nervously looked left and right. No one was looking. "Phew," I exhaled.

I planned to dump my stash of cabbage on the playground, but I forgot. During the afternoon class I put my hand into my pocket and—*oops*—I felt all that raw cabbage. I looked at my teacher, but she did not see it. I pushed the wad of cabbage into my pocket as far as possible so no one could suspect. I planned to dump it in a field after school on the way home.

I forgot again.

Mother Caught Me in My Lie

Mother was checking my pockets that night and discovered the pile of raw cabbage.

"What's this slaw doing in your pocket?" she asked.

I was caught. My nostrils flared. My heart raced. Then I said with all the calmness I could muster, "It was so good, I took extra to eat on the playground."

I still wonder if Mother believed me. I asked her about it when I was grown, but she did not remember the incident. Mothers remember a child's first step, the first tooth and the first word spoken. My mother, however, did not remember my first lie—if in fact she suspected it was a lie. I was not good at lying, so she probably knew. She forgot though. Mothers are like that.

The Importance of the Front-Porch Swing

Other experiences made me think deeply about lying. Some of these experiences occurred in the swing on the front porch of our home in Savannah. One instance I recall involved a lie my daddy told.

Being Grilled in Catechism

I memorized the Presbyterian Westminster Children's Catechism on the front-porch swing. My sister, Martha, and I pushed the old green swing back and forth as it hung by chains from the ceiling. "Squeeeak...erk...squeak...erk..." The swing talked to us as we gently pushed it with our bare feet.

Joining my sister and me on the front porch, my mother asked the first question in the Catechism: "Who made you?"

"God," I said quickly. I always wanted to answer first when the question was easy.

"What else did God make?" was Mother's next question.

"God made all things," one of us answered perfectly.

"Did God make the sycamore tree?" Mother asked, pointing to the tall tree growing in the front yard.

"Yes," I nodded with fervent expression because I deeply believed that God was the Creator of everything.

"Did God make this swing?" Mother pointed to the swing, which needed a paint job.

I was not sure if she was trying to trick me, but I shook my head no and said, "God made the tree, somebody cut it down and built a swing out of it." Mother smiled.

So my instruction in theology proceeded on the porch swing. Mother asked a question and I gave an answer. A correct answer, however, was never enough. She wanted me to understand the words I was spouting so quickly. She believed I understood the thought when I could explain the words.

"What is sin?" was always one of her toughest questions. The answer was a tongue twister, but I could usually spit it out: "Sin is any want of conformity unto, or transgression of the law of God."

"Where do people transgress God's law?" was her next question. She wanted to make me understand the practical meaning of sin.

"Sin is breaking the Sabbath," I said.

Mother waited for more, then supplied it when I hesitated: "Sin is disobeying your mother." Then she reviewed the Ten Commandments, emphasizing, "Don't steal...Don't lie." We never talked about adultery, but I knew that sex before marriage was wrong.

Hearing Lies About Masturbation

One night, sitting on the porch and surrounded by the shield of darkness, my daddy felt secure enough to talk to me about masturbation. Only he did not use the word. As a child I had never heard the proper term.

"Don't play with your peepee," Daddy told me, looking from the porch swing into the darkness. (In our family, I guess the penis was called the "peepee" because of its function.)

"That's what happened to Lewie," Daddy said. He was referring to a young mentally retarded man who lived not far from us, over on Wheaton Street. Lewie was a grown man, but could hardly carry on a conversation. We did not try to talk to him, but just waved when passing on the street.

"If you play with your peepee...," Daddy said. After a pause he continued: "You'll go crazy." He really did not say much more, but that conversation stuck in my mind.

I do not know how old I was before I learned that this was a lie—masturbation does not cause mental retardation. Although it was grossly unfair to use a handicap to try to teach moral values the way my daddy did, that was the way my family handled sensitive issues. Fear and guilt were used to keep a little guy "pure." Parents probably justified lying because of the good they expected as a result. Their greatest concern was that their children do right.

The Truth Can Hurt

Of course, I told other lies in my life. I was a pretty good boy in my mother's eyes, although everyone knew I was not perfect. I lied when I could get away with it.

"You broke my teapot," my sister, Martha, accused me when her prized tea set was broken.

"I did not," was my reply without blinking an eye. No one saw me do it, so I released my sin nature and lied. "I never touched it," I said, reinforcing one lie with another.

When we memorized the Catechism on the porch swing, we inevitably came back to telling the truth. Mother was a "truth teller." If there is weakness in strength, my mother's problem was that she always told the truth—even to the hurt of the hearer.

"Leila," Mother criticized, "You've burned the roast."

"Elmer," Mother said, to put me in my place, "You look dumb when you smile like that." It was her way of trying to motivate me, but saying I looked dumb made me feel dumb. If a mother deals "loser" cards in the game of life, such as always telling a child how dumb he is, it becomes a self-fulfilling prophecy. The child acts as dumb as he sees himself.

Yet, as I have said, Mother also told me, "You're a Towns, you're better than other people." I believed that, too, and tried to be better than the run-of-the-mill people we knew.

Principles to Take Away

1. *The principle of immediate correction.* I learned not to lie by being caught in lies. Mother spanked me as soon as she caught me in a lie instead of postponing it just because it was unpleasant.
2. *The principle of doing right because of who you are.* Mother reinforced the value of telling the truth by saying "No Towns is a liar." Keeping the family name respected was one reason for telling the truth. Keeping the name "Christian" respected by doing right is even more important.
3. *The principle of inward knowledge of evil.* I experienced pangs of conscience when I lied. *I* knew it was wrong, even if no one else knew. I tarnished my self-respect when I lied. It was like splashing mud on myself. I felt dirty when I told a lie.
4. *The principle of deep satisfaction.* As much as I lied and enjoyed the "relief" a lie sometimes gave me, I enjoyed the truth even more because telling the truth made me feel good and clean.

"Deciding never to smoke saved me when pressured—1942"

21

Cigarettes: Not Smoking Your First

You may recall the scene I described involving our Sunday School teacher Jimmy Breland and his warning against smoking. He was standing with several of us boys in front of Eastern Heights Presbyterian Church when he spied a church member tapping a Lucky Strike cigarette on a pack, as a smoker will do just before lighting up.

"Don't ever smoke your first cigarette," Jimmy announced to us with authoritarian finality.

"Why not?" a youthful voice asked.

"It's dumb," was Jimmy Breland's retort. "You waste a lot of money when you smoke cigarettes." He did not moralize or provide any Christian reasons. Jimmy Breland did not smoke, because he was stingy with money. I told you about his never buying a car or a house because he thought he had found cheaper ways to live.

As we stood in front of the church, he turned to me and said, "Would you burn up a dollar bill?" Obviously, I shook my head no. Then he added, "You might as well gather grass off the lawn and roll your own cigarette in a dollar bill and burn up money."

Because of Jimmy Breland's exhortation, I never smoked my first cigarette. My mother smoked when I was young. She came from a family of 11 children, and all my uncles on her side of the family smoked, but I didn't—because of Jimmy Breland.

My daddy came from a family of nine children. He smoked and all my uncles on his side except Uncle Herman smoked. I never smoked, though—because of Jimmy Breland.

The Cat Patrol's Smoke Session

When we were in the fifth grade, the Cat Patrol decided to try smoking. Dwight Arnold carried a single cigarette in his pocket for two days while the group made elaborate plans to smoke it. He sat in class, took it out of his pocket and, carefully hiding it from the teacher, showed it to the rest of us. He grinned. We snickered.

The final strategy was the result of more planning than goes into some bank robberies. We all brought shovels to Dwight's house and dug a tunnel from his backyard under the back of the garage so we could enter without being seen. The garage was covered with tin roofing sheets and was painted red.

We planned for each of us to crawl through the tunnel into the garage and take two puffs on the cigarette. While each of us went for his two puffs, the others played under a nearby pecan tree. They were the lookouts, watching for Dwight's mother. She would tell our mothers if she saw what we were doing and we would all get beatings.

We planned to emerge from the tunnel after taking our puffs and then take a quick swig from a single bottle of warm Coke. The Coke was supposed to cover the smell of tobacco on our breaths. Otherwise we were sure Dwight's mother would smell our breaths and tell our mothers what we had been doing. To get the Coca-Cola, we had walked the ditches of Wheaton Street looking for empty bottles so we could cash in the deposit and exchange it for a bottle of Coca-Cola.

Dwight's older brother, Bobby, had been placed at the tunnel entrance to guard it. Dwight was first. He began the elaborate proceedings by crawling through the tunnel into the garage, lighting the cigarette and taking his two-puff allotment.

Years earlier I had determined never to smoke, as my parents or uncles did. I faced a dilemma, deciding whether to be like my buddies in the Cat Patrol or to be different. Would I smoke? As each of my buddies crawled through the tunnel, I was hoping the cigarette would be consumed from the others smoking it. No such luck.

My Turn

"Your turn," whispered Bobby.

It was now or never. The underground route into the garage was not just a tunnel; it was a "passage of life" into manhood.

I crawled through the tunnel into the garage and saw the lit cigarette. It was placed correctly on a 1939 New York World's Fair ashtray in the middle of a dirty blanket on the workbench. The smoke curled up to the rafters. Sunlight poured through the darkened garage, creating a pattern of contrasting bright shafts of light and darkened corners. The contrasting light and darkness reflected my turbulent mind. Would I live in darkness or light? I had to do something. If I emerged from the tunnel without smoking, the guys would laugh at me. Their scorn was as biting as was my mother's. I had made up my mind, though, that I would not smoke. Now I was confused.

How could I get out of this?

Because I was alone in the garage, I decided to go through an elaborate ruse. I waved and blew on the cigarette smoke, directing it under my sweating armpits to make me smell like smoke. I would deceive the Cat Patrol. Then I retraced my path out through the tunnel and dived quickly for the bottle of Coke, swigging it down before anyone in the gang could smell my breath and determine I had not smoked.

Being My Own Man

That day I experienced the influence of peer pressure. I asked myself if I would do what other people wanted me to do, or if I would do what *I* wanted to do with my life. As we sat around and talked about smoking and conducted a brag session, I lied. I told the

———·——·——·——·——·——·——·——·——·———

I told the other members of the Cat Patrol

I had smoked three puffs. I felt the sin of lying

was okay because I had not committed what

to me was the bigger sin of smoking.

———·——·——·——·——·——·——·——·——·———

other members of the Cat Patrol I had smoked three puffs. I felt the sin of lying was okay because I had not committed what to me was the bigger sin of smoking.

My buddies thought they made their own passage into adulthood unscathed. Dwight's mother had not caught them. They missed the irony of boys acting like men, yet being worried about a mother catching them. Instead of feeling guilty for lying to them, or feeling like a sissy for not taking my first smoke, I felt superior to them for not giving in and following the crowd. Of course, I was not that much of a man. I had not told them what I actually did inside the garage.

It was a warm autumn afternoon. We sat around the roots of the pecan trees in Dwight Arnold's backyard and bragged. We laughed and stretched the truth.

I felt something better than the warm autumn sun. I sensed the satisfaction of being my own man. I had decided not to smoke, and I hadn't. I had done what *I* wanted to do instead of what *they* wanted me to do.

Furthermore, I had refrained from smoking even though the men in my family were supposed to smoke. I was bigger than all of them. That day I decided to live my life the way I wanted to live it, not how others wanted me to live. From that time on I drifted away from the Cat Patrol.

Principles to Take Away

1. *The principle of youthful turbulence.* At the time, I thought I was the only youth who was experiencing turbulent decision-making pressures. The fact is, all children are Beauty and the Beast. They have a beautiful side that only awaits someone such as Jimmy Breland to encourage them to do right. They also have a beast within that will entice them to do things that will destroy them.

2. *The principle of the power of a decision.* We all make decisions that govern our lives. I had made a decision not to smoke, and the power of that decision had kept me from smoking when I faced enormous pressure from my buddies.

3. *The principle of the forks in the road of life.* My decision not to smoke moved me away from the influence of the Cat Patrol. About this time I began a friendship with Arthur Winn that reinforced the principles I learned from good people.

Part VI

Tools That Teach

Our attitudes are formed by the events that make up our experiences. We become strong or weak depending on how we react to these experiences. Most people have more choice about how they react to life than they realize. Poverty makes some people bitter, but others stronger, because they have to fight circumstances just to stay alive. When things and events control us, we become a mere extension of them. In a way, this reduces us to the level of a thing or an event ourselves. We have the power to use experiences as tools. We can learn from them and grow to be greater than our background, or we can be slaves to them.

"My new work attitude brought joy—1943"

22

The Garden: Learning that Work Is Fun

Many people call me a workaholic. Perhaps it is because I don't have any resistance to work. As a matter of fact, I enjoy working. Often I get out of bed in the middle of the night because I would rather go to my desk and work than lie in bed and sleep. I affirm my existence through my work.

Work Before Play

As a young boy I was typically lazy. "Aw, Mom, do I *have* to?" I complained. "I don't wanna!" My reaction was the same as most young boys' reactions today. It is natural for children not to want to work, because it is hard, it is against the flesh and it hurts. Work makes us ache and gives the body pain. So to most youngsters, work takes away the fun in life.

When I arrived home from school, Mother always wanted me to work around the house before I could play. Usually it was not a large job, but she always put work first and play second. The moment I walked into the house she said something like, "You have to dig two rows of potatoes first."

I would do anything to get out of it. I fussed, debated and complained; but I always did it. Mother's dominant will could not be denied.

"Today we're going to put up fence wire for a chicken pen," she announced one day when I arrived home from school. "We're going to grow chickens." We fenced the yard, then built a chicken pen, and for the rest of my childhood we had eggs and, once in a while, fried chicken right from our yard.

Mother was not mean or hard, but work came first. She always wanted me to play with my buddies, and she always made time for that, after work.

Planting Carrots When the Moon Is Full

"The almanac says you plant root vegetables when the moon is dark, and leaf vegetables when the moon is full," Mother said to me one day. "You have to dig up two rows for carrots."

"But Mother," I tried to argue, "all the guys are digging a tunnel under the sidewalk."

The tunnel was really a bomb shelter to protect us from German dive bombers. Of course, it was highly unlikely that any German aircraft could make it to Savannah, and it was just as unlikely that they would target my home in Wagner Heights. Southeastern Shipyard, however, was only two miles away on the Savannah River. That was where World War II landing craft were built. I was convinced that the Germans would attack the shipyard, miss, and a stray bomb would blow Wagner Heights to kingdom come.

"Mother, all the guys are digging this bomb shelter under the sidewalk. Please...pretty please."

"We've got to plant carrots while the moon is dark," she insisted. I could not argue against her logic. The moon did not wait for us, so we had to dig up ground for two rows of carrots.

When I was very young, Mother was much more meticulous than when we were older. She pounded in a stake at the end of each row and stretched a string from one end to the other. The string guided me on a straight path as I dug up the dirt from one stake to the other. Then I had to go back and root out the weeds and dig out all the roots. Each clod of dirt had to be sifted with my fingers.

"If you don't get all the roots out, they'll grow up to choke the carrots," Mother announced with authority. She worked alongside me just to make sure I did a thorough job. It was more than that, though—she loved the dirt.

"See what beautiful carrots we're going to have," she said, pointing to the picture of prize carrots on the seed package.

After we had dug the row and pulled the weeds with our fingers, I raked back through the row, looking for more weeds. Then, turning the rake upside down on its smooth side, I leveled the ground. Next, I turned the rake on end and used the rounded end of the handle to make a long trench from one stake to another. Then, separating the seeds carefully so that not too many fell at one place and choked each other, I planted them evenly, systematically and with exact precision from one end of the row to another.

When we had finally put the seeds in the ground, Mother took the seed package with its glistening, painted orange carrots and placed the envelope on the stake at the end of the row so we would know what we had planted there.

"Can Elmer come play?" David Mixon came to the edge of the yard and yelled. I did not think it was embarrassing to have to work in the garden, but it did seem I had more tasks around the house than all of my buddies did.

"David, you want to swing there in the porch swing for a few minutes?" Mother asked, inviting him into the yard. "Elmer will be finished in two shakes of a lamb's tale." That was her way of saying, "Just a minute."

Playing Football in the Empty Field

An empty field the size of three city lots was located next to our house. Technically, they were not really city lots. The field joined the cemetery, and a deep ditch divided the field from the cemetery. Twice a year men from the Works Progress Administration (WPA)—

a social program to employ men during the Depression—came to clean out the ditch. The field was a great place to play.

I don't know who owned the field, but Sergeant Sullivan of the county police planted a garden there and tended it after work. Each year he plowed the field with his mule and planted a crop there. We knew when a crop had been planted, and we were usually careful not to walk on his freshly planted seed. "He's the law," we said. We

---

One particular day changed my attitude. I was working and my friends were playing. But they were laughing and I was griping. <u>If I decide to like work, I'll have more fun in life</u>, I thought.

---

also knew that each fall he plowed it for planting next spring, and that we did not have to worry about seed being in the ground during football season.

Seven or eight guys gathered in the plowed field. My dad had given me a rubber football. We kicked off, then ran at each other as fast as we could, which was not very fast in the plowed field, and we hurled our bodies at each other. Because the ground was soft, I don't remember anyone getting seriously hurt. I do remember that we got covered with dirt the way a baby is covered with too much talcum powder. The field was more sand than black dirt. Dirt was imbedded in our hair, our underclothes, under our fingernails and spread around our eyes. The dirtier we were the better.

Changing My Attitude About Work

One particular day changed my attitude. I always hated having to work in Mother's garden. Play was fun, but work was definitely NOT FUN. On this particular afternoon, Mother had me digging up some weeds and turning over the soil. There I was, picking the roots of weeds out of hardened dirt clods, my fingers getting filthier by the moment. The guys were yelling in the plowed field. I looked at them through the hedge, or when I had to go to the chicken coop to get another tool. I could see the guys running, playing and rolling in the dirt.

They're just as dirty as I am, I thought. *They're dirty...I'm dirty...* They were sweating and getting tired, and so was I; but they were laughing and I was griping. The thought was becoming more than just an idea.

I thought about the two scenes. We were both getting dirty, we were both sweating and we were both using a lot of energy. *Why can't I have as much fun at work as I have at football?* I wondered. The question intrigued me. I remembered that I was usually more tired after playing football than I was when I worked for Mother in the garden. After we played football we usually took a hose, washed off, then lay down in the grass to let the warm sun heal our bodies and restore our strength. Lying in the sun was just as much fun as playing football.

One day after I had been working in the garden I was extra dusty, just as the baby covered with too much talcum powder. So I took the hose and washed myself from top to bottom and went to lie in the grass. The sun was just as warm after working in the garden as it was after playing football, and I had just as much fun lying in the grass.

This feels like football, I thought. The sun was warm and the grass was therapeutic. What was happening to my body, however, was not as significant as what was happening in my head. I analyzed why I did not like to work, and concluded that it was all in my thinking. I did not like to work because of what I would later call "attitude."

If I decide to like work, I'll have a lot more fun in life. That was a profoundly life-changing thought for me. I concluded that if I treated work the way I did football, life would be happier. As I turned over in the warm sun to let its rays heal my aching back, I decided—not just in my head, but deeper within my experience—that from now on I was going to like work and make it fun.

The Supreme Test

The supreme test came the next day. I had been playing football in my dreams all during school. When I got home Mother reminded me, "Don't forget you're going to cut the grass today." Cutting grass at my house then was nothing like it is today. Today a kid has an electric starter on his gas engine, or at worst a pull cord on the power mower. Then he uses a power trimmer for the edges. Raking is unnecessary because grass clippings are caught in plastic bags. By today's standards, grass cutting is clean, easy and comparatively effortless.

Not when I was a kid. We had the old-fashioned reel mower that had to be pushed. And when you are only 75 pounds pushing a 35-pound mower, it ain't easy. Usually, I cut a section and rested awhile, lying in the grass or going inside for iced tea. Six sections of grass had to be cut at 107 Wagner Street. A section was located on both sides of the front stairs, a third on Wagner Street, divided by flower gardens, and three more on the side yards, divided by the vegetable garden and tree roots. None of the sections was very large, but I still had to get that heavy mower moving six times. I also had to overcome my mental obstacles to get started again after finishing each section.

When I decided to like work the day before, I had in mind work that took only 10 or 15 minutes. Then I would go and play football. Cutting the grass, however, was different. That usually involved all afternoon, and I had no time left for football.

I was fortunate on this particular day. The guys were not playing football next door so I had no mental distraction or enticement.

"I'm going to do the best job I've ever done in my life," I said as I pulled the lawn mower out from under the house. The rake and shovel were stuck in the blades, so it took a little effort to slide them out and get ready for work.

I cut all six sections without taking my usual breaks. Probably each section did not take more than four or five minutes, but to a little guy that is an eternity. "This is a great job," I bragged to myself, looking at one of the small sections. Every blade of grass seemed evenly cut, like piling on a wool rug. I got down eye level with the grass to see if I could find one blade out of place. I spotted a few, and with the hand clippers manicured them into place. Then I eyeballed the hedge. *It's got to be straight*, I said to myself. Next I trimmed the edges with hand clippers as carefully as Jimmy the barber trimmed around my ears. Then I ran my eye down the edge of our broken sidewalk, just to make sure not one single blade of grass was touching concrete.

Great, I said internally, *that's a perfect line of grass.*

Each time I finished one section of the lawn, I went back to compare it with a previous section and to glory in my achievement. Just as the architects of the pyramids in Egypt must have taken pride in their achievements, so I took pride in the lawn at 107 Wagner Street.

As I lay on the front lawn admiring my work, I thought, You know, this yard is so good, if President Roosevelt could see it he'd have me come and cut his White House lawn.

Expressing a desire for excellence that seems to be inside nearly everyone, I said, "This is the best cutting this lawn has ever had!"

Discovering Satisfaction in Work

I write this and laugh at myself now, realizing that as a young kid I meant exactly what I said about having given that lawn the best cutting job it ever had. As I lay on the front lawn admiring my work, I thought of the president of the United States driving down Wagner Street. *You know,* I thought in my childish way, *this yard is so good, if President Roosevelt could see it he'd have me come and cut his White House lawn.*

So lying in the middle of our own manicured lawn, I envisioned how I might tackle the White House lawn. I did not know about the fence around the White House, and I had no idea how large it was. As a boy I thought the White House must have been about as large as some of the lawns in Gordonston where the rich people of Savannah lived. *It would probably take me all day to cut the White House lawn,* I imagined.

After I finished all six sections of our lawn, I raked them carefully. Then, because Mother had a compost pile, I made sure to put the clippings in the pile and cover them with lime. When the job was all done, I went back to the front lawn, lay flat on my back and placed my hands under my head, and stared at the sky through the leaves of the sycamore tree. I enjoyed one of the most satisfying experiences I can remember. It was more fun than playing football, better than winning in football. I, Elmer Towns, had accomplished one of the greatest feats in life. I had cut the lawn at 107 Wagner Street better than it had ever been cut in its life.

I lay there for a long time reveling in my accomplishments. As a grown man I look back on that lawn-cutting experience. Little did I know that this one experience would change my attitude toward work. I would discover satisfaction in work on other occasions, but the manicured lawn on that day had a lifelong influence.

Principles to Take Away

1. *The principle of controlling my attitude*. Early on, I had a bad attitude toward work so I hated it. Later, after changing my attitude, I enjoyed work; and the change had a large and growing influence on my life. I learned that I could get more out of life by changing my attitude.
2. *The principle of identifying with work.* When I identified with the lawn, I took pride in perfectly manicuring it. Motivation to do a good job comes naturally when the job becomes the person who does it. I do a better job when it is "my lawn" and "my garden."
3. *The principle of job satisfaction.* Happiness can be achieved in doing a good job, in completing a task satisfactorily.

"I was grateful for running water—1950"

23

Water: Gratitude Is the Rarest of Virtues

I think gratitude is one of the most important attitudes in life. The ability to be grateful can make you happy, keep you from being ill, turn you into an optimist and help you get along with people.

When teaching, I repeatedly tell my students, "Gratitude is the least remembered of all virtues, and the acid test of character." I don't know where I learned that phrase; I think it came from a literature course in college, perhaps from Charles Dickens.

I hope I never take running water for granted. When I turn the handle and splash clean water on my face to shave, I thank God for water. When I flush a toilet and clean water washes down the bowl, I am grateful for water that runs into my home.

Doing Without Running Water

We did not have running water in my grandpa's house in the country. A pipe stuck out of the ground at the bottom of the back steps. The spigot on the pipe spouted water about six inches into the air before it fell into a metal washtub partly submerged in the sand.

"Get a bucket of water for your mother," Grandpa yelled. I retrieved an empty bucket off the water shelf in the kitchen or off the sink on the screened-in back porch. The old home had a galvanized sink on the back porch, but no spigot, so a bucket of water was left beside the sink. The bucket in the kitchen was for cooking and the bucket on the back porch was for washing ourselves. That bucket full of water was left on the counter so we could wash our hands and faces.

"Wash outside in the tub and save yourself some work," Grandpa exhorted me. So before I came inside, I stuck my head under the spout of water from the pipe, and plunged my face and hands into the tub set into the ground. On really hot days, I dipped my whole head under water, shaking off as much excess water as possible before running up the stairs to wipe myself dry.

"We need two buckets," Grandpa yelled. "Y're holding up supper." When the two buckets were empty, I knew someone had poured water from one bucket upstairs to the empty one instead of fetching more water. It did not make any difference. Both were empty. Supper was cooking. Grandpa or Mother never tried to find out who failed to get water when the bucket had been emptied. It was easier to yell, "Elmer, get some water." My mother used a demanding tone, "Fill both buckets."

"Somebody drank it all and didn't fill 'em up," I complained. But Mother did not argue.

"Your legs are younger than mine." I heard that from her many times while growing up.

When I got to the bottom of the stairs, I hung the empty bucket handle over the upturned spigot and turned it on. It seemed to take forever to fill a water bucket. Sometimes I played toy soldiers in the sand while waiting. I could win a lot of wars waiting for the bucket to fill. Sometimes I went "from victory to victory" and won several wars before the bucket overflowed into the tub.

"Hurry up with that water!" someone yelled. It took two hands to lift the handle of the heavy filled bucket over the upturned spout.

When I got to the stairs, I walked up each stair one at a time. I stepped up, then pulled the overflowing bucket up to my level; step up, pull up. It always seemed arduous and took a long time.

Time should not have meant anything to a little boy. "Hurry up with that bucket" always had a threat that if I did not get it there

---

"Grandpa," I asked one day, "why don't you get longer pipe and run water to the kitchen?" I was proud of my insight for figuring out that such a feat could be done, and I wondered why Grandpa had never thought of it.

---

promptly, I might get a spanking. Inevitably, I spilled water on the back steps or the floor. The house, however, was not constructed of hardwood floors as are many modern homes. The steps were just made of unfinished lumber and in some spots had cracks in the floor, so the spilled water just flowed on through and onto the ground below. A little boy could peer down through the cracks in the floor and watch the chickens under the house.

Advising Grandpa

"Grandpa," I asked one day, "why don't you get longer pipe and run water to the kitchen?" I was proud of my insight for figuring out that such a feat could be done, and I wondered why Grandpa had never thought of it.

"It's an artesian well," Grandpa explained, sitting on a block of cut firewood in the sandy backyard. We had no grass in our backyard. We kids had to chop with a cotton hoe any grass that tried to grow in the backyard. The sandy yard was packed and smooth—Mother even swept it with a broom. The backyard was our second living room.

"If we got a pipe up to the kitchen, I wouldn't have to carry water," I explained to Grandpa. He laughed; I don't know if he was proud of my insight or laughing at my naiveté.

"This pipe is 76 feet into the ground," he explained. "That's all the deeper Bobby Mercer could drill." Bobby Mercer had drilled the hole by using a gigantic wheel that screwed a water drill into the ground. They did not have access to a power drill; they used a hand drill that operated only by the force of extreme physical strength.

Grandpa explained that a gigantic river flowed 76 feet under the ground, and the water pipe was tapped into it. Then he explained, "The pressure of the river will only push the water about two feet above the ground." Grandpa told me they once ran a pipe up to the back-porch sink, but nothing came out. The water would not flow another 10 feet to the back porch.

I nodded my head as though I understood. "What about Uncle Henry?" I said. "He's got water all the way to the second floor."

Grandpa laughed again, "He's got an electric pump that pumps the water all through the house."

I nodded my head because I did understand that. Uncle Henry had electricity because he lived on the south side of the Black River Swamp, but Grandpa did not have electricity. My parents had installed running water in our home in Savannah when I was three years old; but Grandpa never had running water in his house.

Today, when I turn the faucet, water pours into the basin without a bucket and I am thankful. I am not a complete optimist—every once in a while I reach for the faucet and think, *What if nothing comes out?* But the water has always come.

After I was grown, I went into the refugee camps along the Mekong River in Thailand, where the Cambodians fled the Khmer Rouge in 1977-1978. The *Reader's Digest* described that the mass destruction and collapse of civilization in the cities of Cambodia happened as a result of the uncivilized Khmer Rouge. When the escapees said that even the water supply was destroyed and nothing flowed from the water pipes, I thought about the young people of America. How would they react if they had no running water?

Going to the "Branch" for Water

"Go to da branch for water," Grandpa told me one summer when it did not rain much. The underground river must have flowed low that year because we did not have enough pressure for the water to come out of the faucet at the bottom of the stairs. The water merely dribbled out of the spigot into the bucket; it took an hour to fill one bucket.

"Get your wagon," Grandpa said. "You'll have to get water from the branch." We called the stream about 500 yards from the house the "branch." I pulled my red wagon filled with empty buckets across the backyard, through the pasture and down a narrow wagon trail into the woods. The wagon trail only ran into the water of the creek and out again. No bridge had been built over the branch.

I pulled my wagon to the branch, carefully choosing my route to make the return trip easier. The trip seemed to take forever, maybe half a day; but probably it took 10 or 15 minutes for the round trip.

Pulling the wagon right into the branch, I watched the water wash the dirty wheels. I usually spilled some water out of the buckets on the trip back to the house, sometimes returning with the buckets only half filled. I never started out from the branch with just half buckets of water, however, because then I returned to the house with even less water.

I learned to lean forward to let my weight pull the wagon instead of just using my muscles. I learned that slow was better than fast because I lost less water. I learned that the long way around the edge of the pasture was easier than the shortcut across the soggy bog.

Rain Was Our Friend

A bad storm erupted one Sunday afternoon at Grandpa's place. The sky turned black. Lightning flashed and some pine trees in the woods were splintered. An oak limb punched a hole in the roof of Uncle Paul's room. Buckets of water poured from the sky.

I pouted. "I wanna go outside to play," I complained on the screen porch, sticking out my lower lip.

"That rain is your friend," Grandpa philosophized. "Tonight there'll be water at the spigot and you won't hafta go to the branch."

I sat and watched the rain a long time. It seemed to rain into the night and I wondered if Grandpa was right. When everyone went inside, I could not wait any longer. I ran out into the rain and down the steps to turn on the spigot. Only a dribble. I forgot about it until the next morning and I heard Grandpa bellow from the kitchen.

"Elmer—get a bucket of water from the spigot," he hollered. Sure enough, when I turned it on the water flow was as strong as ever.

Saturday-Night Baths

People laugh about Saturday-night baths, but they were a ritual at Grandpa's. Usually I sponged off every night in the metal tub partly submerged in the sand under the spigot. Saturday night, however, we all took a warm bath in a washtub in the corner of the kitchen.

The black woodstove was heated with cut pine logs for cooking, but on Saturday morning it warmed water in the reservoir at the side. Because the reservoir could not hold enough water for everyone, all the buckets and some large roaster pans of water were placed on top of the stove so we could have enough warm water.

I am especially grateful for hot water because we did not have it either at 107 Wagner Street in Savannah, although we did have water piped into the house. I did not live in a house with hot water until I went to college.

Taking a bath in a large round washtub is an art form and is a psychological trade-off. First we took a washrag (we never called them washcloths, because they were old raggedy towels cut into small pieces). I stood naked beside the tub and got the washrag wet and soapy. I soaped my face, arms and body, right down to my waist. If two or three cousins, such as John and Paul David O'Cain washed with me, we all soaped down, then rinsed off our heads and arms, all of us standing naked around this one washtub. Then the oldest to the youngest stepped into the tub, soaped down the rest of our bodies, then rinsed. Usually, three or four of us used the same water because of the need to haul and heat the water. Today, when I stand in the hot shower, I thank God for little things such as hot water—hot running water.

College—"Decayed Elegance"

My first Saturday at Columbia Bible College was on September 13, 1950. It was a rainy afternoon in Columbia, South Carolina, as I stood in Legster Hall, Room 401, looking out the window over the campus. I shared the room with Bob Yount. He was away from the room just then, and the room was gray, reflecting the cool rainy weather.

Then I heard something I had never heard before. Pipes were knocking throughout the building. Someone had turned on the furnace, and the hot water made the cold pipes pop and bang. Then I felt heat coming through a radiator—I had heat in my room! I never had a heated bedroom at home. I always slept in a cold bedroom and used plenty of covers. I never understood why Bob Yount asked me when I was moving into the room, "What d'ya bring all those

As hot water was splashing over my head, I thanked God through unashamed tears: "Thank you, Lord. I may never have it this good again."

blankets for?" Then he made a crack about my being from the South. Bob Yount was a Yankee from Michigan.

That chilly afternoon I felt the flow of warm air on my face as I looked out on that chilly rain. I began to cry.

Why am I crying? I asked myself. I knew I was not homesick. At the time I did not understand my emotions, and I was afraid of my tears. Now that I look back, I realize they were tears of gratitude. As a college freshman, however, I was ashamed of my tears. Grown men did not cry. I surely did not want my roommate to see me in that condition. To hide my tears I went down the hall to the bathroom and took a shower—a hot shower.

The shower stalls were old World War II rejects from an army base. The tin sides were rusted, the base was mildewed and dirty curtains were hung for privacy. Some of the guys on my floor were full of criticism for "the hole," as they called the shower room. To me, however, hot water was a luxury. As hot water was splashing over my head, I thanked God through unashamed tears: "Thank you, Lord. I may never have it this good again."

Legster Hall was more than 100 years old. It was as old as my grandpa's house in the country; but electricity had been added to the men's dorm, water pipes ran on the floor next to the hall baseboards, and heating pipes were laced through the building from floor to floor.

"Decayed elegance" is how I described that ancient old lady of a building. My spoiled floor-mates called it a fire trap and a "flea bag hotel"; but I loved the place. I could not believe God had given me such a wonderful place to live for a whole year.

Even if I were to run out of money and have to go home, at least I had experienced one wonderful year with a warm radiator in my room and hot running water just a few steps away.

Principles to Take Away

1. *The principle that gratitude produces character.* Why is gratitude the acid test of character? Because it does not come naturally. It must be taught to children. "Say thank-you," we tell the little girl. But she shakes her head no. My mother made me write thank-you notes, or go to someone's house to offer appreciation for something the person did. All things flow to and from the child. Children must be taught what others do for them. The clinched baby's hand at birth must be pried open so the baby can say, "Thank-you."

2. *The principle of Christian gratitude.* A true understanding of grace makes us appreciative of God's sovereignty and goodness. "Not by works of righteousness which we have done" (Titus 3:5). To bow the head and gratefully acknowledge thanksgiving to God from a grateful heart is the beginning of character. It is the foundation of worship.

3. *The principle of the gratitude approach to living.* I am grateful for appliances, houses, cars, books and a world of other things. Someone else invented them; someone else sacrificed to give them existence. If I appreciate them now, then I can live without them if they were ever to be taken from me.

4. *The gratitude-satisfaction principle.* By learning to be grateful for things, I develop satisfaction and happiness apart from them. Although things may make me happy, they are not the basis of my inner satisfaction.

"Being on time is my passion"

24

The Clock:
Be There, and Be on Time

When I was in the first grade, the teacher sent home a report card to inform my mother about my progress. I had earned not a single *A* on the card, but neither did I have any *F*s. My school record shows a transcript of average exploits, in everything except attendance.

I was never late in 12 years.

My mother took the card and pointed to the tardy column. "I will send you to school on time, and you will have lots of time to get there," she said. She paused to emphasize the seriousness of this matter, then said with equal seriousness, "If you are tardy, I will beat you to death."

Now I knew Mother did not mean she would physically kill me. I was flesh of her flesh, and she loved me. Most mothers, though, have a weakness for saying things they don't mean when they are irritated. Like the mother who tells her child, "I'll slap your face into next week"—we know it is physically impossible to remove the face of a child by swiftly swatting a human hand. Mothers exaggerate that way though.

At any rate, the way Mother said it, I believed the unpardonable sin that would damn a person's soul to hell was to be late for school. For 12 years in public school, I was never late one time. You can go back and check all the report cards, you can check Waters Avenue School, Chatham Junior High School and Savannah High School; the record stands impeccable. Elmer Towns was never late. That is quite an accomplishment—not for me, but for my mother.

A Close Call in High School

At least I was never late for school on record. One early winter morning in high school, my good buddy Art Winn and I were riding our bicycles to school. He stopped at the barber shop at the corner of 37th and Waters Avenue to get a haircut, and he had to wait for two men ahead of him. When Art finally climbed into the chair, it was only a few minutes before 8:00 A.M. School began at 8:20, at which time I would be late. Mother's threat years earlier echoed in my mind: "I'll beat you to death." This was in the eleventh grade; I had had an unblemished record for 11 years.

I stewed and tried to read a magazine. Inwardly, I fumed about being late. Finally I could stand it no longer. I ran out of the barber shop, jumped on my bike and peddled furiously at sprint speed to Savannah High School. About a block away from the school I heard the bell ringing—the 8:20 bell that told me I was late.

I knew that my life had collapsed, but I kept going. I cut across the ROTC drill field, slammed my bicycle into the others, and in swift, rhythmic motions locked the front wheel to the bicycle stand. As I ran into the hall, I experienced something I had never felt previously. The hall was empty. I could hear the buzz of students in their homerooms. Roll calls were being taken, and I could hear the students' responses: "Present," "here" and sometimes "yo."

I quietly opened the door of Room 106—my homeroom—where Mr. William B. Lane rallied us in opening exercises each morning.

Opening the door slowly, I tried to sneak in. Standing in the ~~doorway~~ doorway I realized that the angels in heaven loved me. Mr. Lane was not there. My legs went rubbery. My racing heart, in a death grip with

---

My racing heart, in a death grip with guilt, felt as though it would explode. Like a baseball player stealing home in the last game of the World Series, I was gloriously safe. Mr. Lane had not called the roll.

---

guilt, felt as though it would explode. Like a baseball player stealing home in the last game of the World Series, I was gloriously safe. Mr. Lane had not called the roll.

A Perfect Sunday School Record

I had the same perfect record in Sunday School. When I began attending Sunday School at the Eastern Heights Presbyterian Church on the third Sunday of September 1938, I was not yet 6 years old. Because I began attending public school when I was 5 years and 11 months old, Mother also let me begin Sunday School at the same time. To her, Sunday School and public school were no different.

"I want you to get one of those Sunday School pins like the other good children," she stated flatly. "You will not miss Sunday School and you will be there on time."

Eastern Heights Presbyterian Church awarded a Cross and Crown pin—made of white porcelain adorned with gold trim and red and blue letters—to each student who had a year of perfect attendance. It was an expensive-looking pin, not a cheap trinket. I was required to bring back a note certifying my attendance at another Sunday School when we went on vacation. My mother could send a note to excuse me up to twice a year when I was sick, and I could still get the pin.

Erin Towns, however, allowed no excuses. She explained very

carefully her rules of the game, the rules by which I was expected to play. "I don't believe in sending a note for being sick," she said. Perfect attendance meant one thing and one thing only. It meant that I was in Sunday School 52 times a year. Because Mother was the rule maker, she could never be the ruler breaker. She lived by her own rules, which meant I went to Sunday School without fail. I never missed.

"I'm going to send you to Sunday School in Mr. Breland's truck," she said, making it sound like a threat. "When you get there, don't go out and play in the fields." She told me that if I "cut" Sunday School and did not get perfect attendance, "I will beat you to death."

Just as in public school, I did not know if she was kidding or not. So for 14 years I never missed Sunday School, not even once for sickness.

Eastern Heights Presbyterian Church also sent home reports that included a column for tardies. Mother told me she was sending me to Sunday School on time, and I better not have a mark in the tardy column. I was not to go out into the fields to play on my way to Sunday School, or to goof off in any other way.

Playing Sick

In the first two or three grades, no problems occurred. Jimmy Breland came down Wagner Street in his shiny black Jewel Tea truck. I waited on the front porch, then ran down the steps when he arrived. He opened the back door of the panel truck, where I sat on the floor. Week after week, I rode to Sunday School in Jimmy Breland's truck.

About the third or fourth grade, I got wise to what my friends were doing. I heard the stories about how they stayed home "sick." They just told their mothers they were sick, even if they were not. I decided to try it.

"I'm sick, I can't go to Sunday School," I announced to Mother one Sunday morning. She did what good mothers do. First, she put the back of her hand against my forehead to see if I had a fever. The back of a Mother's hands are magic. They know whether you are sick or are lying.

"Hmmmmm...," Mother said, doubt scrolling across her forehead. Then she went the thermometer route. You have seen a Mom do it, before they invented the new thermometers. First, she snapped it three or four times to force the mercury into the little ball at the bottom of the thermometer. Then she stuck the glass thermometer past my tonsils till I gagged.

Mother was not concerned about my failing health;

she was concerned about my truthfulness.

"You're not sick, you're sickening," she announced,

going into the bathroom to get medicine.

When Mother pulled out the thermometer she formed another, "Hmmmm..." The lines in her forehead deepened into a frown, then a scowl. I could tell that things were going from bad to worse. She was not concerned about my failing health; she was concerned about my truthfulness.

"You're not sick, you're sickening," she announced, going into the bathroom to get medicine. We did not have a medicine cabinet in our bathroom. Instead, four wooden orange crates standing on end became shelves on which the family kept our medicine and "cure-alls." Mother rummaged around, whistling as she looked for a certain brown bottle. The whistle made me nervous. I thought she ought to be concerned about my sickness. When Mother was happy, or up to something, she whistled.

"Here it is," she said as she pulled the brown glass bottle with an oil-soaked label out of the back of the orange crate. Across its front were imprinted simple words—Castor Oil.

"If you're sick enough to stay home, you need to take castor oil." Uncapping the bottle, she put it under my nose. I gagged. Who wouldn't? Not only is castor oil nasty, but I would also go as far as to call it filthy; castor oil brings out all the gases of your stomach. I smelled it, and gagged again.

I knew what this meant—three tablespoons full. She ladled it down my throat without a chaser and I gagged again at the taste.

She gave my sister, Martha, orange juice to cut its nasty taste, but not me. I was Erin Towns's pride and joy. She made sure my character was sterling pure, sincere, without guile and without an orange juice chaser.

"I'll go...I'll go...I'll go," I said. Then to make sure she saw my sincerity I added, "And I'll be on time. I won't play along the way."

Mother did not make me go to Sunday School; she made me *want* to go to Sunday School.

Attending Sunday School When I Had Mumps

Once I was actually sick and should have stayed home, but the attendance record was more important than the boy. I had a temperature and my face was flushed, but Mother sent me to Sunday School. Immediately after I got home she put me to bed. That evening my cheeks puffed out, my jaws hurt and my eyes watered. I really was sick. Mother had sent me to Sunday School when I had the mumps.

Obviously, I stayed home from Waters Avenue Public School that week. Something that does not happen today occurred. Dr. Eagan, our family doctor, visited our home. We bought a prescription and I dutifully swallowed it. Whether it was the medicine or the mumps just running their course, the fever went down and the pain in my jaws vanished.

By Saturday I was allowed to sit on the porch in the sun, and to stray into the yard. I was dressed warmly, wearing two pairs of socks, long corduroy pants and a red plaid flannel shirt. Over all this I wore a scratchy, wool bathrobe. A faded khaki scarf was wrapped twice around my neck. To top it off, Mother pulled a stocking cap down over my ears. Erin Towns took no chance of my getting a chill, but I could have sweated to nothing in the interim.

"I think you can go to Sunday School," Mother announced the next morning. She began to rationalize. "You've got perfect attendance." That was foremost in her thinking. "Mumps are contagious before you swell up, but not after the swelling goes down," she continued. "No one knows you've been sick," she concluded, rationalizing that the other mothers would not get upset at her.

So Mother bundled me up again, just as she had the day before:

two pairs of socks, heavy long pants and flannel shirt. She did put a wool sweater on me instead of the bathrobe. She pulled the stocking hat down over my head, commanding, "Don't let anyone take this off."

"Yes'm," I said, nodding my head dutifully.

She told me to sit by the door when I got there, not next to anyone. Finally, just in case a little swelling was left in my cheeks, she told me that if anyone looked at me, "Suck in."

Long after I was grown, people asked my mother if she really sent me to Sunday School when I had the mumps. They hear the story of her telling me to "suck in," and have difficulty believing it. When someone criticized her for sending me to Sunday School when I had the mumps, she said, "You like the way he turned out, don't you?"

Breaking My Attendance Record

The first time I missed Sunday School was in my sophomore year at Columbia Bible College, and I absolutely was not at fault. After 14 years of perfect attendance, I agonized at the thought of missing. Then I went through withdrawal pains after I finally broke the record and was absent. My perfect attendance that had begun at 5 years and 11 months of age was broken in my nineteenth year. Because I had to attend a full year to receive one year's perfect attendance, I only have 14 bars on my Sunday School pin.

In college I was assigned to a gospel team that ministered at a country church. The team was led by an older student who drove the school van and did the preaching. His name was David. I forget his last name. He had blonde curly hair and usually wore a stupid-looking bow tie. I was the song leader, and four girls were on the team—one was the piano player and the other three formed a vocal trio.

Early that week we met together to plan the Sunday morning schedule. I was given a list of the songs I was to lead. I had to practice to make sure I could sing each song. The girls' trio selected two songs that fit the theme of the service. The piano player was Jackie Houston, one of the gals I thought was cute—so much so that I constantly flirted with her. Although we were the same age, she thought I was too young for her. She flirted with the upperclassmen, ignoring my advances.

I am describing Jackie because she became the main culprit in the activity of the morning. We decided at our planning session that David was to check out the van. We planned to meet him at 9:00 A.M. in the lobby of the women's dorm. David was to drive to the country church, which was only 15 minutes away in a rural area. Sunday School started at 9:45 A.M. I would be able to attend and thus keep my perfect record intact.

The morning service began at 11:00 A.M, which was the standard time for most preaching services. We emphasized at our planning session that we were not involved in the Sunday School program, only the church service. As a matter of fact, we emphasized two or three times that I was not leading the singing in Sunday School, the trio was not singing in Sunday School, Jackie was not playing the piano in Sunday School and David was not speaking in Sunday School. We all, however, were planning to attend Sunday School.

A Tardy Team Member

At 9:00 A.M. we were all gathered in the girl's dorm lobby except Jackie. I had been there about 15 minutes because I was always early. "Where's Jackie?" someone asked. Lorraine, one of the other girls, phoned up to her room. Lorraine's face grew pale. She walked over to explain. "Jackie went back to sleep after breakfast because she wasn't feeling well."

I panicked and said, "But we'll miss Sunday School." No one seemed to care but me.

Lorraine explained that Jackie would be down as soon as she was dressed. We all sat down in the lobby to wait. I started to fidget and the more I fidgeted, the more irritated I became. I probably went beyond irritation to anger, maybe even to wrath.

I was frustrated at the dilemma I faced. If I told them I was breaking a 14-year record, they might laugh at me. It was a common point among preachers to make fun of Sunday School attendance pins. Many people seemed to have depended upon their attendance pins to gain entrance into heaven. After all, I was attending Columbia Bible College and was now a mature Christian. I could not tell them about my Sunday School pins, could I?

Associated Reformed Presbyterian Church was located two blocks from Columbia Bible College, a church I visited on several occasions. *If I broke into a dead run, I could be there in less than three minutes,* I thought. My attendance could be counted at the Associated Reformed Presbyterian Church Sunday School. Jackie, however, could walk down the stairs at any moment, and if we arrived at the Sunday School in the rural church on time I could still be counted.

So I sat in the hard leather chair of the school lobby, weighing this decision with eternal implications. Should I run and put in an appearance at the Associated Presbyterian Church to keep my Sunday School pins activated? Or should I wait for Jackie and hope I could get to the rural church on time?

Late for Sunday School; On Time for Church
The story has only one conclusion. By the time Jackie fixed her hair, got dressed and came down, it was 10:30 A.M. When we arrived at the rural church it was 10:45, and Sunday School had ended. We were on time for our assignment in the worship service and we ministered for the Lord. I wish I could remember how I felt that day, standing in front of the crowd as I led the singing. I wish I could remember if God used me, or if I was so agitated that I grieved the Holy Spirit.

I do remember, however, sitting in the lobby of the women's dorm fretting and stewing about Jackie Houston. My unblemished Sunday School record was broken that morning, and it was one of the major crises in my life at the time.

Lessons Learned

Now, many years later, I care not at all for that Sunday School record. So I have learned in life that the things that are absolutely major at the moment are really small when viewed from a distance. Some of the things that used to make me the angriest are not worth a second thought.

I dated Jackie Houston once. I do not remember if it was before or after the event. We never discussed her being late. After Ruth and I were married, I was an usher at Jackie's wedding and Ruth was a bridesmaid. We have remained friends. She probably does not know about her role in breaking my attendance record.

In afterthought, perhaps God was sovereignly behind the scenes, crushing my legalistic attendance expectations and cutting me off from some of those traditional comfort zones in which I used to hide. Perhaps God was making me more pliable in His hands so I could be more innovative and creative—traits I could not have developed had I remained in the comfort of my accomplishments.

Principles to Take Away

1. *The compulsive principle.* Once you value time, you realize that lost time cannot be recaptured. It is lost forever. Therefore, the ticking clock becomes the drumbeat of our lives. We either march to its cadence, or it tramples us. Although Sunday School attendance built character in me, it also enslaved me to tradition. Jackie Houston unwittingly broke that compulsiveness.

2. *The clock-produces-character principle.* Once we value time we are no longer selfish, because we prize something outside ourselves. When we properly use time, we allow it to produce character in us. Character is repeatedly doing the right thing in the right way in the right attitude for the right purpose—because it is right.

"Unfulfilled dreams taught me motivation"

25

The Bomb: Dreams that Are Not What They Are Cracked Up to Be

Uncle Johnny and I went for a walk down the Atlantic Coastline Railroad tracks. When we returned, he called me into his garage and showed me a large 100-pound bomb. "Wow!!!" I exclaimed. Although the thing was only a dummy, I was impressed. It was the first bomb I had ever seen up close. It had a round smooth nose. Although it was called a 100-pound bomb, it weighed only about 25 pounds because it was empty.

My eyes became large and my "wanna" got selfish. I wanted that bomb. I wanted it bad.

CHAPTER TWENTY-FIVE

"Can I take it out in the yard to play?"

"Sure."

Even a 25-pound bomb is heavy for a little boy. It was as tall as I was. I dragged the dummy bomb up onto the washstand and dropped it like a World War II high-altitude bomber over Germany.

Thump! It hit the ground and fell over on its side. I dragged it up onto the washstand again and yelled at the top of my squeaky voice, "Bombs away!" I whistled the sound of the noise I had heard falling bombs make in the war movies. Then I scrunched up tongue and lips to simulate an exploding bomb in enemy territory.

Uncle Johnny told me that the bomb came from an Air Force training airplane that had crashed about a mile from his house on the other side of the potato field. At first I did not believe him. Then when I heard the ladies talking about it, I knew it was true.

Years later, I decided Uncle Johnny had found the bomb and kept it even though the Air Force from Hunter Field in Savannah had been looking for it. Maybe that is why he let me carry it home.

"You mean I can really have it?" I grinned and thanked him a million times. Late that Sunday afternoon when it came time to head back to our home in Savannah, I pulled the dummy bomb into the backseat of the car with me and my sister. "Thank you, Uncle Johnny," I said again, waving good-bye.

Dropping the Bomb

All the way home, I dreamed of pulling that bomb up into the tree house in the pecan trees in the backyard. I could see myself dropping it as though I were a bombardier over Germany. I debated whether to drop it parallel to the ground, the way they dropped bombs out of a B-17. But if I did that, I thought, the bomb would not have time to turn perpendicular on the target in its brief flight from the tree house to the ground. So I decided to hold the bomb perpendicular and drop it straight down.

"You can't drop it tonight," my mother told me when we got back to Savannah. "It's too dark to play outside tonight."

That was it. Even though the American planes could bomb at night, Mother said no. No night bombing mission was to take place from the pecan tree in our backyard.

That night I dreamed of flying a B-17 over Germany. I avoided the enemy by exploding flak, but held the Flying Fortress steady.

Then we released the hundred pounder and I closed my eyes to see the bomb sailing majestically toward the earth. I heard its long whistle, and imagined the fear it struck in the hearts of the enemy. When it struck earth, the flash of light was as terrible as lightning— I blew up an ammunition factory. The boom of the great bomb's

---

All the way home, I dreamed of pulling that bomb up into the tree house in the pecan trees in the backyard. I could see myself dropping it as though I were a bombardier over Germany.

---

explosion was followed by a sound like the long rumble of thunder.

The next day in school I daydreamed all day. Dismissal time at 3:00 P.M. could not come soon enough.

"Ugh." I strained to lug my fantastic new toy up into the tree house. The sharp, sheet metal fins were easy to grab, but they cut my young hands. I tried to climb the boards nailed to the tree trunk for a ladder while carrying the bomb on my shoulders, but I could not do it. It was too bulky to carry up to the tree house.

A rope was the answer. I tied a rope around the bomb and although the rough rope burned my hands, I was finally able to pull the rusting bomb up to the tree house. At last I was ready. For 24 hours I had dreamed of this awesome moment. I had something no other boy in America had. I had a 100-pound bomb of my very own.

I stood on the edge of the platform we called a tree house, the bomb standing next to me. I did not want to just push it off. The launch had to be more glorious and victorious than that. I yelled, "Bomb bay doors open!" On my command the doors opened and the chilling, subzero wind rushed into the belly of the great Flying Fortress.

"Bomb ready," I yelled for everyone in Wagner Heights to hear. I looked down into our backyard, searching for a target.

"Target ahead!" I yelled, alerting my crew.

"Bombs awa-a-a-y!" Using all my might I suspended the bomb out over the imagined target and released it.

Thump!

That was it. There was no fearsome whistle, no long, graceful arc in the bomb's descent, no explosion as it struck its target. Nothing but a dull *thump*.

In short, the bomb's 10-foot flight was disappointing. I dropped it, it fell 10 feet, it hit the ground and it fell over on its side.

Expectations Extinguished

My anticipation drained as if biting into a rotten peach. I expected a rush of excitement and energy, but I felt nothing. I tried it several more times, adding more sound effects. I whistled the way a real bomb sounded. I made what I imagined to be bomb explosion sounds. I even built a dirt factory below the tree house and practiced demolishing dirt targets. All my efforts, however, had the same disappointing effect. The results simply did not equal my expectations.

I dropped the bomb eight or nine times that afternoon. Then, like a small child, I began to lose interest. The next afternoon I dropped it two or three times. When my buddies came to visit, I dropped the bomb some with them. Soon, however, the excitement of the bomb was extinguished. It lost all its addictive hold over me and I went on to other projects. Later, when my buddies wanted to drop the bomb, I tried to talk them out of it.

The bomb taught me that I was happiest when I dreamed of something, not necessarily when I achieved it. Unfulfilled anticipation is a greater motivation in life than is saturated fulfillment.

Principles to Take Away

1. *The principle of anticipated happiness.* We think many things will make us happy, but when we get them, they often don't deliver. I was happier when I dreamed of playing with the bomb than when I actually played with it.

2. *The now principle.* I had to learn that happiness is now—not looking back at yesterday or dreaming about tomorrow. If

I live in the past, or always dream about the future, I miss *today*. Today is the yesterday you will look back on tomorrow. Today is the tomorrow you dreamed of yesterday.

3. *The bigger-than-life principle.* The bomb taught me that some things are bigger than life. The bomb was literally bigger than I was, yet its physical size was out of proportion to its impact on my life. Although I had a hard time learning it, the lesson was that things are not bigger than real live people.

"Picking cotton taught me about brotherhood"

26

Picking Cotton: Picturing God

Where does a little boy get his view of sovereignty and divinity? How do children learn about God?

We learn about God from teachable moments that flash like lightning on a dark night. We remember the brilliant flash, and the fingers of light are etched on our minds. We forget the darkness surrounding the flashes of light, however, for nothing in darkness demands recollection.

I learned about God from Sunday School and by memorizing the Presbyterian Westminster Children's Catechism. I formed opinions from Bible stories and theological debate in doctrine classes. But on a hot, sunbaked cotton field on my grandpa's farm in South Carolina I got a glimpse of God I could not have obtained in any formal class.

Working Alongside the Sharecroppers

I had been picking a row of cotton along with several black children and their fathers. I don't remember where their mothers were. Usually I could pick 100 pounds a day, for which I was paid the same as the other pickers—a penny a pound. A dollar a day was a lot of money for a little boy, but it was backbreaking work. Bobby Johnson, a middle-aged black sharecropper on my grandpa's farm, picked his row, then helped pick my row so I would not get behind. Bobby could pick more than 200 pounds a day—twice what a child could do.

As Bobby and I got to the end of the row, we all sat on a mound of plowed dirt, our aching legs stretched into the row for relief. I could see the church building for the blacks on the other side of the branch at the east end of the property. (Remember, we called the stream or creek that bordered the farm the "branch.") I asked Bobby why we (meaning white folks) did not go to their church, and they did not come to ours. (Children are color blind at birth; they have to be taught distinctions.)

The Color Distinction
"You folks is Presbyterians," Bobby philosophized, "and we's Baptist." The sun glowed red like an ember in a fireplace.

The other black men cautioned, "Careful, Bobby...he's Cap'ns boy." They called Grandpa "Captain," and they did not want Bobby to be in trouble with the boss.

Bobby was the preacher at the Baptist church for the sharecroppers, and black people came from all around to hear him elevate the glory of God every Sunday, beginning about noon. Resting at the end of that cotton row, Bobby lifted a little boy into heaven just to let the child feel the glory of God.

"We's both believe in God," Bobby explained, wiping sweat from his face with a dirty white handkerchief, then tying the white cloth around his neck to catch the perspiration. Then he quoted Psalm 104 and expounded the text, just as though it were Sunday noon.

The Awesomeness of Psalm 104

"'O Lawd my God, thou art very great,'" the black man recited, giving reign to his resonant voice. "Dat's how King David magnified de Lawd." Bobby quoted the *King James* impeccably. He knew Psalm 104 by heart.

Bobby explained how they worshiped God.

"We goes to de church to spread praise on God —like

spreadin' buttuh on de biscuit —cause it's so good."

He explained how they worshiped God. "We goes to de church to spread praise on God—like spreadin' buttuh on de biscuit—cause it's so good." I understood that simple analogy. It was preaching a small boy could comprehend. I liked it.

"'Thou art clothed with honor and majesty,'" Bobby continued from the Psalm, his voice lifting triumphantly over the white cotton bolls. "God gets up in de mawning and slips His arms into a bettah coat than I've got. He's got a coat of honor and majesty. It ain't got no holes and de lining ain't torn."

"Amen! Da's it," echoed the field hands.

"'Who coverest thyself with light as with a garment.'" Again Bobby's resonant voice quoted the richness of the Psalm. "God reached for de sun and stuck both legs in de sun like a man pullin' on his pants. And de sun fits de Lawd just fine. God wraps His body with sunbeams from top to bottom, and He's shiny and dazzlin'. God is *sumpn'* when He gets dressed up!"

"Amen!" The chorus of voices again supported Bobby's eloquence.

"Come on, preach it," they encouraged.

"'Who stretchest out the heaven like a cuht'n.'" On a roll now, Bobby continued to cite the *King James* flawlessly. "Dis means God grabs de heavens up dere." He pointed to the sky. "God says, 'I need a cuht'n to hang up to get me some privacy,' just like me and my wife hang a cuht'n in de livin' room so d' chillun don't watch us sleep. God needs a little privacy. See—de' sky, He's on d'other side, an' dat's de Lawd's cuht'n. Dat sun is His garments an' He's coverin' us wit' Himself by de sunshine."

I have always believed in the sovereignty of God—that He is great and powerful, and that He is the author of this earth. He is immense. I have also believed in the imminence of God—that He sees everything I do.

"'Who maketh the clouds His chariot,'" Bobby continued. "God's got a cah bigguh'n a Buick...bigguh'n a Cadillac. God's cah takes Him anywhere He wants t'go. He walks into d'front yard, jumps in a cloud as big as He wants, and cranks it with a key—not a hand crank like I got. God turns on d'radio in His cah—it's car got everything. An' He goes everywhere. He don't need no road."

"Amen!" a field hand shouted in agreement.

Then Bobby called me by the name the blacks used for Grandpa. "Cap'n," he said, "you gonna be a preacher." Bobby was the first to tell me I was going to be a preacher.

"'Who walketh upon the wings of the wind.' God's a wind walker." Bobby's black face broke into a huge smile that radiated the contentment of God. The white dust on his face was streaked with perspiration.

"He don't burn His feet on de hot dirt like us. God walks on de wind, which is cool. His feet never hurt an' He never has to rub 'em. He never gets tired an' He never has t'sit down t'rest. God jes' walks...and walks...and walks. He does it on de wings of de wind. The breeze on our face comes to us on wings—jes' like de wings of a bird...soft wings...gentle wings...smooth wings...tenduh wings."

"You Gonna Be a Preacher"

Then Bobby called me by the name the blacks used for Grandpa.

"Cap'n," he said, "you gonna be a preacher." Although that was not the first time I had thought about serving the Lord, Bobby was the first to tell me I was going to be a preacher. Today I know I had a call of God, and not just because of Bobby; and I know that at a later time I surrendered to preach. From my earliest memory, though, I had always thought about preaching, and I always saw myself as a preacher.

"Cap'n...yo heart's tender to God...you gonna be a reveren'," Bobby told me that day.

"I want to come hear you preach," I told Bobby. I never did visit that little country black Baptist church on the other side of the branch, and I never did hear Bobby preach. Yet that church influenced me through its members and its minister as they worked the fields of my grandpa's place.

I never forgot the day someone told me I was going to be a preacher. It was good news, and the message made me happy. I stretched out on the dirt of that cotton row on Grandpa's farm and thought about how the message "fit." I wanted to be a preacher.

Principles to Take Away

1. *The different-thought principle.* The sharecroppers taught me to think about God in a way that was different from my Presbyterian Sunday School training. Although I was taught to reverence and fear God, they taught me to enjoy God.

2. *The first-call principle.* Bobby Johnson did two things for me. He told me that God had called me to be a preacher, a thought I never forgot. He also taught me to magnify God and people who want to serve Him. I wanted to serve the God of Bobby Johnson.

3. *The brotherhood principle.* Picking cotton, I learned the brotherhood of the human race. Although our cultures may be different and our skins a different color, underneath we are brothers.

"Stories brought the world to me"

27

The Front Porch: Listening to Grown-Ups

Storytelling was the glue that tied together the values and attitudes of my boyhood. I grew up before the advent of television, and we did not even have a radio in the house until I was in the third grade. Before we bought our radio, we went to Aunt Ina's and all the kids sat on the floor while the adults sat in chairs as we listened to the one station in town.

When I lived on the farm in the summers we had no electricity, so we could not listen to a radio at all. On the hot summer evenings we children sat on the front porch and the adults talked, usually telling stories. Only a Southerner can understand that it was too hot to sit in the house on summer evenings, especially after the sun went down and the heat radiated down from the attic.

Our Summer After-Dinner Schedule

Shortly after dinner, my father went out to the front porch and sat on the swing. Although the swing could hold two people, he always sat by himself. Raaaaak...raaaaak...raaaaak, the swing rasped like a rusty file scraping a dull ax.

Krik...et...krick...et. The crickets auditioned in harmony about an hour before sundown, and I heard them until I went to sleep. Living close to the ocean, the loon always reminded us of its presence. Sometimes we could hear the hoot of an owl. We always got a flashlight and tried to find it. There was something special about owls, perhaps because they did not come around too often.

Daddy did not talk much, at least to the children. He sat in the swing and smoked cigarette after cigarette. Once the darkness descended, we could look across the street and see the red embers of Mr. Conway's cigarette. We knew he could also see the embers of my dad's cigarettes.

"Turn out the living room lights," Daddy told me as I came out the front screen door. We were too poor to have a screened-in porch, so we usually sat in the darkness because the mosquitoes did not bother us as much in the dark. As soon as the porch light was turned on, the bugs swarmed in from everywhere, followed by squadrons of mosquitoes.

Across the street, the Conways also sat in darkness, until the last year of the war. In 1945, at the end of World War II, they had their front porch screened in. It changed their whole life. Because of the screens that kept out the mosquitoes, they could read the paper by a small reading light. They also stopped talking and telling stories when they began to read.

Our neighbors to the south were the Hoffmans. Mr. Hoffman was not a drinking man, so he always had more money than we had. Mr. Hoffman was the first to screen in his porch. Then he winterized it, adding aluminum jalousie windows—the glass windows—which I always thought ruined his front porch. The porch did not have heat in the winter so he could not use it in cold weather. The heavy jalousie glass windows did not open wide enough to admit much of a breeze, so their porch was too hot to sit in at night.

So the Hoffmans never sat on their porch. When he thought he had the best of both worlds, he had neither of either.

Stories Brought the World to Us

One evening as we sat on our front porch in the darkness, Daddy began to tell a story. "A B-17 bomber crashed in the Savannah River

I learned a lot about what worked and what did not work just by listening to my dad's criticisms and affirmations. I learned by listening to stories.

marshes today," he said. Then he told us at length about how Air Force personnel came to the White Hardware Company where he worked, looking for supplies to take into the marshes where the plane had crashed. During high tide the marshes were covered with water, and a flat-bottom boat could be maneuvered about. At low tide the marshes became a muddy bog, and the boat got stuck if it did not get out before the tide went out. That evening's story was a long one because it included a detailed description of the various items Daddy sold to the Air Force for their plane recovery.

"You fellows can't use rubber boots, you'll get stuck in the mud," Daddy told them. "Send in young men with just their pants on, no shoes or socks, so they can wade through the mud."

I learned a lot about what worked and what did not work just by listening to my dad's criticisms and affirmations. I learned by listening to stories.

When the dishes were done, Mother came out to the porch. We did not keep a rocking chair on our porch as did some of our neighbors. Usually we pulled a wicker rocking chair out of the living room onto the porch for the evening. If I was sitting in the rocking chair, Daddy said, "Get up and give your mother the chair."

We always jumped up when an adult came onto the porch. Usually I sat on the top step and leaned back against the round pillar holding up the porch roof. Sometimes I straddled the banister rail, and other times I sat on the stairs.

We sat on the north end of the porch because the south end was filled with potted plants. Mother watered them in the afternoon sun. The flowers had long branches and weedy leaves, and were a festering place for mosquitoes. So instead of sitting among the plants, my brother and sister and I sat on the stairs or somewhere near the swing.

As I grew older, I always kept my bicycle on the front or back porch. Riding into the yard during the day, I lay down my bike on the ground or once in a while leaned it against a tree. When coming home from the last trip of the day, however, I swung off with a one-step motion, picked up the bike, carried it up the stairs and leaned it against the house on the porch. The handle bar rested against the house wall, holding the bike upright. For some reason, Mother thought that if the bike was put on the porch no one would steal it, but if it was left in the yard someone might walk off with it. Her rationale was, "If they come up on the porch, we'll hear them." So because the bike was leaning against the house, we did not lean against the wall. The bike covered all the available wall space.

The stories I heard on our front porch helped explain why there were good times and bad times, and somehow that made the bad times seem more tolerable.

Principles to Take Away

1. *The value of stories principle.* I learned from the stories told by older folks. They talked about their childhoods, their jobs and their relatives. They told funny stories and sad stories, short stories and long stories. They told true stories and some stories they wanted us to believe were true.

2. *The story-dream principle.* Stories taught me to dream. They taught me the difference between good and bad dreams, what to long for and what not to desire. Stories brought the world to Wagner Heights. I lived beyond my geographical limits through the events I heard others describe.

"Dreaming of cherries"

28

Cherries and Chicken Noodle Soup: Hating What You Love, Loving What You Hate

As a boy, I often saw pictures of banana splits with big red cherries on top. I wanted a banana split throughout my boyhood, but I never got one until I was a teenager. Even more than the banana split, I wanted a ripe, red, luscious cherry. We were too poor to ever have banana splits or sundaes or milk shakes, all of which came with red cherries on top. I dreamed of maraschino cherries. (I am older than cherry Cokes are.)

Although cherries seemed to be reserved for the rich, one cherry tree grew on my grandpa's farm. Unfortunately, it produced sour cherries. I dreamed of the ripe-red, rich-red, big-red, sweet-red cherries—the kind that came in a wonderfully shaped bottle. Once in the grocery store I just sat down in the aisle and stared at the bottles of red cherries. Even as a kid I understood the meaning of lust.

Fantasizing About Red Cherries

So I fantasized about red cherries. I used to fantasize about what they tasted like. I spread cherry jelly on toast, so I had an idea how cherries might taste. Once I ate cherry ice cream, and it was marvelous—heavenly, just as I imagined. I imagined, though, that maraschino cherries would taste much better. It is amazing how you can imagine what something tastes like if you have never had it. Everyone said the big fat cherries were good, so I thought they must taste wonderful. Perhaps anticipation makes you want some things more than you really do want them.

Then came the day when I had my first red cherry on top of a sundae. I closed my eyes and rolled it around in my mouth. I sucked the sweetness out of it. Then I chewed and swallowed. The cherry was not bad, but neither was it as good as I imagined. *Maybe the next one will be better,* I thought. Several months later I ate my second cherry, and it did not taste any better. I kept thinking they would improve. They had to; cherries were the most desirable fruit in the world. I even told a friend that Satan used a cherry to tempt Eve in the Garden of Eden.

I started my first paper route when I was 11 years old. I earned about $9 a week, if I collected from everyone. That was a lot of money to a boy who had had so little for so long. What was I going to do with all that money? The first thing I wanted to do was to buy everything I had never had before. A popular phrase in the South stated that a little child who had too much money "burns a hole in his pocket."

The Ultimate Prize
I thought about eating all the cherries a little guy could want. So in the summer of 1944 I peddled my bike to Womack's Super Market, the store where mother did most of her shopping. I knew exactly where the bottles of cherries were shelved. To my surprise, I found

both red and green cherries. The green ones were artificially colored; they were meant for parties. I did not want them. I wanted red cherries.

The large jars were about 12 inches tall, very narrow and cost $1.35. That was a lot of money on my salary. The small jars cost

---

I did not know then that much of life is like our dreams of a warm bath. Once we get in, it's not so hot.

---

about 80 cents, and that was expensive enough. In those days a can of vegetables cost less than a dime, but cherries were exorbitant because they were a delicacy. Today, the price of vegetables has increased, and cherries have become comparatively more reasonable.

The cherries were stacked in perfect rows on top of each other—beautiful red cherries in clear jars, packed in a crystal syrup. I picked up a large jar.

"Whatcha gonna do with dem cherries?" Mr. Womack asked as I paid him $1.35. "Yo momma know you buying these?" he asked, fully aware of our financial problems.

"I got a paper route," I boasted. "This is my money."

"You gonna eat 'em all?" Mr. Womack continued his line of questioning. A boy possessing that many cherries was unusual.

"Yes, sir."

I stuffed the tall bottle into the canvas bag that held my newspapers. Sitting down on the corner of Wheaton and Cedar streets, I leaned against a sweet gum tree and unscrewed the cap from the jar of cherries. I popped the top cherry into my mouth, and rolled it around my tongue. I put the cap on the bottle, expecting to make the cherries last a long time. Involuntarily, though, I chewed the cherry and swallowed it in one fluid motion.

I'll suck the next one longer, I promised myself as I again unscrewed the cap.

These are really good, I said to myself, chewing and swallowing the second, and third and so on.

When I finally "killed" the bottle, it was time to deliver my papers. I took the tall bottle home to show my mother because it looked so unique.

The cherries fermented in my empty stomach. I did not get sick, but I was queasy. The more I thought about the cherries, the less I liked them. I was too young to know the adage: You can get too much of a good thing. I did not know then that much of life is like our dream of a warm bath. Once we get in, it's not so hot.

As I was growing up, I learned that I could lose my yearning for some things I deeply desired (like chocolate and cherries), by getting too much of them.

A Change of Desire

I learned to like other things that I hated at first. Like chicken noodle soup. I used to gag on chicken noodle soup. I had seen pots of chicken noodle soup simmering on the stove. The soup was covered with slime. The yellowish broth boiling up from the chicken bones reminded me of chicken intestines. I did not like the idea of eating chicken guts.

Yuck, I thought, and decided I did not want any.

"Mmmm," Mother said, pouring herself a bowl of chicken noodle soup. She ladled down a liberal portion with a large soup spoon, and smacked her lips.

"Yumm," she said, trying to entice me.

I shook my head and said, "No ma'am." This scenario was repeated several times. Because I had made up my mind I did not like it, I wasn't having any. "I don't like chicken noodle soup," I said with finality.

Fall came to Savannah, carrying nippy winds and moisture in the air. The naked trees lifted their empty branches to the sky. The pecan tree in the backyard offered a little guy no protection from the misty rain, so I was playing in the kitchen. The pot-bellied stove in the center of the kitchen kept us all toasty warm.

The aroma of cooking food filled the kitchen. Something cooking on the stove smelled delicious. "Smells good," I said to Mother.

"Only enough for me," she answered. Mother had always given me the best piece of watermelon, the first dish of pudding. She had always made sure I got something first. So I was puzzled when she said, "Only enough for me." But she ignored my inquisitive look.

The aroma from the simmering pot made me hungrier. I liked what I smelled. Then Mother poured chicken noodle soup from the pot into a bowl. I watched her spoon a mouthful, and I wanted some.

"Mmmm," she smiled, knowing the battle was won.

"Can I have some?" I shyly asked. My humble spirit reflected a new attitude toward chicken noodle soup. I had surrendered. She poured half her bowl into mine.

The first spoonful was great. *How can I not like this?* I thought. *Think of all the good soup I have missed.* I scraped my spoon on the bottom of the empty bowl and asked for more.

"There's no more."

"I sure like it...now."

Mother went to the mantel where the family kept its money. She took out a nickel and a penny—six cents—and sent me to the little store two blocks away. I bought one can of Campbell's chicken noodle soup and ran through the chilly rain all the way home. I cut off the top with a can opener and poured it into a pot.

"Mmmm," mother said, sipping her hot chicken noodle soup.

"Mmmm," I responded.

I had made a decision not to like chicken noodle soup, and my mind controlled my taste buds. I had actually thought it was yucky. But on a cold autumn day, a chilly little boy smelled something that was pleasant. He wanted it, only to find out it was chicken noodle soup—something he did not like. When he changed his mind, his physical response changed.

Principles to Take Away

1. *The principle that decisions control acts.* I learned that there is power in a simple decision. I was missing a lot of good things in life because of bad decisions. By changing my mind, I could be happier.
2. *The principle of simple pleasure.* We think exotic things such as maraschino cherries will give us satisfaction, but that is not true. Some simple things in life such as chicken noodle soup can bring more pleasure. We could all be happier if we settled for simple pleasures.

"The big kid"

Epilogue

With Respect to Our Unrelenting Memory

We remember the stories of our childhoods with what we believe to be accuracy because we cannot lie to ourselves. So the stories in the preceding pages are true according to my memory. When I revisit my boyhood home, however, the house is not as big as I envisioned, and when I see photos of former friends, they are not the same as I remember them. Yet both the way I remember the events of my life and the truth about what really happened are part of my story, and therefore are a part of me.

Your memory may be just as faulty when you retrace your own story. Still, I pray that what you recall and what you discover about your memories will edify you, as my memories and my discoveries have edified me.

As the baby busters, or Generation X, have discovered, truth can be discovered in stories. They often want to know how the world has been perceived to work for others, whether or not it is the absolute truth.

My story is the way the world has worked for me.

"Erin and Elmer Sr."

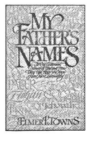

Discover What the Bible is All About.

What the Bible Is All About™ is one of the all-time favorite Bible handbooks. This classic 4-million copy best-seller and its family of resources will help you stamp out biblical illiteracy.

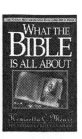

What the Bible Is All About

Henrietta C. Mears

The classic 4-million copy best-seller takes the reader on a personal journey through the entire Bible, covering the basics in a simple, understandable way.

Hardcover • ISBN 08307.16084
Paperback • ISBN 08307.16076

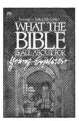

What the Bible Is All About for Young Explorers

Frances Blankenbaker

The basics of What the Bible Is All About in a graphic visual format designed to make the Bible more approachable for youth.

Hardcover • ISBN 08307.11791
Paperback • ISBN 08307.11627

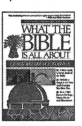

What the Bible Is All About Quick-Reference Edition

This easy-to-use Bible handbook gives a brief overview of the people, events and meaning of every book of the Bible. Includes over 1,000 illustrations, charts and time lines.

Hardcover • ISBN 08307.13905
Paperback • ISBN 08307.18486

What the Bible Is All About Video Seminar

Elmer L. Towns

Here, in just three hours, Dr. Elmer Towns presents an outline of God's plan for the ages. He shows how this plan is established on six key "turning points" in history. Armed with a clear understanding of these foundation points, students can turn to the Bible with a deeper understanding of its content.

Video Seminar • SPCN 85116.00906 (Package includes book, reproducible syllabus and 2 video-tapes.)
Audio tapes • UPC 607135000815

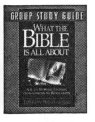

What the Bible Is All About Group Study Guide

Wes Haystead

A teaching companion for the best-selling classic. In 5 to 10 weeks you will give your students an overview of the Bible with concrete illustrations and clear commentary. Includes reproducible study sheets.

Group Study Guide • ISBN 08307.16009

Gospel Light

These resources are available at your local Christian bookstore.

What the Bible Is All About 101 Group Study Guide Old Testament: Genesis–Esther

Henrietta Mears

Here's a 13-session study that takes your class through some of the most important—and yet least-understood—books of the Bible. Students will also get a clear picture of Jesus as He is revealed throughout the Old Testament.

Manual • ISBN 08307.17951

What the Bible Is All About 102 Group Study Guide Old Testament: Job–Malachi

Henrietta Mears

Introduce your students to the poetry and prophecy of the Old Testament—and what it teaches us about God's plan for all time-fulfilled in Jesus Christ.

Manual • ISBN 08307.17978

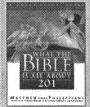

What the Bible Is All About 201 Group Study Guide New Testament: Matthew–Philippians

Henrietta Mears

Here are the foundational parts of the New Testament from the birth of Christ to Paul's letter to the Philippian church—encouraging students in their walk and challenging them in their faith.

Manual • ISBN 08307.17986

What the Bible Is All About 202 Group Study Guide New Testament: Colossians–Revelation

Henrietta Mears

As you take your class through the last 16 books of the Bible they'll see how all of the Scriptures are woven together by God into a beautiful tapestry that tells about His plan for all time.

Manual • ISBN 08307.17994